MW00415476

What leaders are saying about Scott Wilson and *IDENTITY*:

I doubt if you've read a more unvarnished, transparent, and unfiltered leadership book than *Identity* by my longtime friend Scott Wilson. When I read this book, I laughed, I cried, I hurt, I celebrated, I learned, and I grew. No doubt, you'll do the same. I recommend this book not just to you, but to all the leaders in your life. You'll love it, but more than that, it will change you.

> —Sam Chand, Leadership Consultant, Author
> of *Harnessing the Power of Tension*

Scott and Jenni were born for this! The thirty-one years they've been in pastoral ministry were for this moment and this calling . . . to help lead pastors become all God has called them to be. I can tell you right now that Scott and Jenni are the greatest spiritual father/mother combo in America. That's a fact.

> —John Maxwell, No. 1 *New York Times* bestselling
> author, coach, and speaker who has sold more than
> twenty-four million books in fifty languages

Very few people challenge me or encourage me like Scott Wilson. He is a pastor of pastors, a leader of leaders. You can't be around Scott and Jenni very long without getting God ideas! If you're ready to grow, personally and organizationally, I can't imagine a better mentor or spiritual father. Ready, set, grow!

> —Mark Batterson, Lead Pastor of National Community Church,
> Washington, DC, *New York Times* bestselling author

Leaders are learners. It is inherent in a leader to improve. So, in their quest to grow, they seek out the best. They look for people with fresh eyes, those who see what they don't see, so they can become their best. Biblically, this is played out by Jethro and Moses. Jethro saw what Moses didn't see. Scott Wilson is a modern day Jethro. He has pastored, and he knows what it's like to live in the trenches. He's built a ministry that's esteemed and respected. If you're a pastor, borrow from Scott's eyes. He'll help you see better, he'll help you be better, and he'll help you become better.

—Gerald Brooks, DD, DCL, Founding Pastor of Grace Outreach Center, Plano, Texas, Author of *Understanding Your Pain Threshold*, *What I Learned, While Destroying a Church*, and *The Building Blocks of Leadership*

Want to grow your church to one thousand plus? If so, I am pleased to recommend Pastor Scott Wilson and his organization: Ready, Set, Grow. They will help you apply biblical principles and practical strategies that will result in fulfillment of Isaiah 54:2-3. So, get ready to enlarge the place of your tent, stretch out your curtains, lengthen your cords, and strengthen your stakes. You will expand!

—Walter Harvey, President, National Black Fellowship, Assemblies of God

IDENTITY

The Search That Leads to Significance and True Success

SCOTT WILSON

AVAIL

CONTENTS

Introduction
Lifting the Lid

You were born for a purpose. No matter who you are, no matter what you've done, no matter what background you come from, God has a magnificent purpose for you. You aren't an accident (though your parents may have thought so), and you're not a random collection of molecules that somehow evolved over billions of years. You are God's special creation—a child of the King and His valued partner in the greatest enterprise the world has ever known.

This isn't a new thought, but it's amazing how few of us actually believe it. It doesn't matter if you can quote passages and teach others about our identity in Christ if that truth hasn't truly penetrated your heart. Do you believe you are who God says you are? Can you declare with David: "I am fearfully and wonderfully made; your works are wonderful, I know that full well" (Psalm 139:14)? Do you really believe, like Peter, that "[God's] divine power has given us everything we need for a godly life through our knowledge of him who called us by his own glory and goodness" (2 Peter 1:3)? Everything? Yes, everything. And does your heart explode with joy because you believe that "we are

God's masterpiece. He has created us anew in Christ Jesus, so we can do the good things he planned for us long ago" (Ephesians 2:10, NLT)?

God has given you a new, revolutionary identity, as well as the skills, gifts, and talents to fulfill the purpose He put in your heart.

The grace of God accomplishes many things. Certainly, it frees us from the penalty of sin, but it also grants us the awesome status of being God's adopted, beloved children. It empowers us to accomplish anything and everything God puts in our hearts to do. As His children, we have the unspeakable privilege of seeing Him use us to accomplish His life-changing, eternity-defining goals. Each of us plays a vital role in revealing God's glory to the people of the world, to shine like lights in the darkness, to point the way to salvation by faith in Jesus, and to establish His kingdom on earth as it is in heaven. Nothing can come close to that purpose—no title, no amount of money, no pleasure, and no power over others. Don't misunderstand: there's nothing in the world wrong with titles, money, pleasure, and power . . . unless they are in the center of our hearts. When our hearts are filled with the love, wisdom, and power of God, He may give us those things, but we'll hold them loosely because they don't matter as much as He does.

In kids' movies, television shows, books, and in school, the constant message is, "You can be anything you want to be!" For instance, in one of Elsa's songs in *Frozen*, she asserts,

> *It's time to see what I can do*
> *To test the limits and break through*
> *No right, no wrong, no rules for me I'm free!*[1]

---

1 "Let It Go," Idina Menzel, Frozen, Songwriters: Kristen Anderson-Lopez / Robert Lopez, Walt Disney Music Company, 2013.

Sounds good, doesn't it? Kids love to sing along, and little girls imagine themselves as Elsa. It's beautiful, and it's powerful . . . but it's a poisonous lie. You can't be anything you want to be. I'm not trying to discourage you. I'm just being honest with you. In fact, I want to encourage you that you shouldn't even try to be "anything you want to be." You should focus your full attention on becoming everything God wants you to be. That's something you can fully become—you were uniquely gifted and made for it—and your God-given purpose is a far bigger and better goal for you to pursue.

Other pursuits bring only temporary fulfillment, and they leave us always craving more. But pursuing God's purpose has a very different impact on us: We experience the joy of seeing Him use us to meet needs, change lives, and make a difference in countless ways, and the joy multiplies as we grow in grace. Our goal every day is to align our hearts with who God says we are and align our choices with the purposes God has given us to accomplish.

The messages of our culture tell us that we can determine our identity. It's our choice, and we fulfill it by our grit and determination. But a biblical identity is discovered. Like a treasure hunt, we search the Scriptures to find the diamonds of truth that shine with brilliance to tell us who we are and how God wants to use us. We spend time with mature, secure believers who reinforce what we see in the pages of the

> **Our goal every day is to align our hearts with who God says we are and align our choices with the purposes God has given us to accomplish.**

Bible—and we let these messages sink into the deepest crevices of our souls where doubts, fears, and shame have lived too long.

Our grasp of who we are in Christ determines how much we embrace our God-given purpose. Self-concept is either a launching pad to trust God to use us in incredible ways, or it's a lid that limits our capacity for growth and impact.

VOICES

Negative or distracting voices can easily drown out God's message of love and purpose. Children are sponges. They soak up the words and the moods of their parents and other adults. To some degree, all of us have grown up in flawed families because no one escapes the effects of the fall in this life, even those who have made commitments to God. I consider my childhood to be about as wonderful as anyone's I've ever known, but I sometimes overheard my parents worry about money, I saw the hurt because they felt misunderstood, and I watched them absorb some of the pain as they counseled people who were suffering. As a child, I incorporated those fears and doubts into my worldview, and they were reinforced in many ways in my interactions at school and at church.

When I was a freshman in high school, I went out for the basketball team. I played pickup games with my friends, and I thought I was pretty good. Tryouts included every boy in every grade, so I walked into the gym with seniors who looked a lot more like grown men than I did—I'm pretty sure some of them even shaved! From the way they were dressed, I could tell almost everybody but I had played in leagues before. The first drill was a weave, when three players pass the ball and run behind the one catching it, and doing it over and over again. It was,

I learned later, the first and simplest drill in the game, but I'd never seen it before. I was petrified.

When it was my turn, I told the kid behind me to take my place. Finally, I was at the end of the line. It was now or never. I passed the ball, ran behind the guy, and walked out of the gym. The message that was burned into my heart that day wasn't, *I'm no good at the weave drill.* It was, *I'm no good at anything! And I never will be.* That conclusion became a stronghold that effectively locked out the truths of God's love and purpose for me. In that moment in the gym, I had been vulnerable, and I was traumatized by self-doubt. My self-perception of sweeping incompetence seemed like an undeniable fact.

I never wanted to be hurt like that again, and I never wanted to feel that level of shame again, so I built walls of self-protection. The walls certainly limited my vulnerability, but they also prevented me from being honest about the pain, so God could bring healing.

It was twenty years later that God gave me insight and healing about the damage done in the gym that day. The memory had haunted me for all those years, but God graciously showed me:

You just didn't know how to do a drill. That's all. It's no big deal.
It doesn't say anything about who you are and My plans for you.
Your interpretation of the event is a lie. Reject it. My plans for you
haven't changed at all. It's time to move on.

I felt immense relief. I told God, "I reject the lie and receive the truth that You've prepared me with every skill I need to accomplish Your purposes. No more lies, no more walls, no more limitations." I realized that if God's purpose for me was to be the next Michael Jordan or LeBron James in the NBA, He would have given me the skills for that. I think it's safe to assume that wasn't God's master plan for my life, but His plan was still right in front of me, all day every day.

THE PROMISE OF PERFORMANCE

Undoubtedly, the most pervasive and persistent lie the enemy tells us is that our significance is based on our performance. If we do enough, if we succeed enough, if we impress people enough, we're valuable. If not. . . . This is the way the world works, but it's not the way God's kingdom operates. In school, business, organizations, and sadly, many churches, we live by a formula that seems unshakable: We *do* to prove what we *are*. But in God's economy, we *are*, so we *do*.

Does the simple transposition of short words really matter? Yes, it's night and day! If we believe our performance is the basis of our identity, when we're doing well, we feel proud, superior, and confident. But when we've failed or our efforts aren't appreciated, we feel ashamed, inferior, and confused.

The order is crucial. If we aren't convinced that we're loved, forgiven, and accepted by the grace of God and not by our good works, we'll be driven to perform, and we'll always worry that we haven't done enough . . . and we'll look over our shoulders to see if others are performing better than we are. Their success becomes a threat to our security.

> **Does the simple transposition of short words really matter? Yes, it's night and day!**

SPIRITUAL FATHERS AND MOTHERS

I don't struggle to have faith in God. My struggle is in having faith in who God says I am. This isn't a fleeting issue. I've been wrestling with it my entire life. As I've talked to people—from pastors to new believers—I've seen that I'm not alone in this struggle. I gave my heart to Jesus when I was just a boy, but it has taken a lot longer to give my mind to Him. God is obviously very patient, because He continues to reveal His love and purpose, and He persistently reminds me of how He sees me. Through the prophet Isaiah, God told His people,

"Can a mother forget the baby at her breast and have no compassion on the child she has borne? Though she may forget, I will not forget you! See, I have engraved you on the palms of my hands."
—Isaiah 49:15-16

Do you know any nursing mothers who forget they have a child? No, me either. God is saying, "You're always on My mind." God loves us so much that He has our names tattooed on His hands where He can't miss them! God isn't playing hide and seek with us. He delights to reveal Himself to us and affirm our relationship as His children. In his first letter to the Corinthians—who needed a lot of correction about their performance and pride—Paul assured them that the Spirit longs to impart life-transforming truth:

What no eye has seen, what no ear has heard, and what no human mind has conceived—the things God has prepared for those who love him—these are the things God has revealed to us by his Spirit.
—1 Corinthians 2:9-10

If we ask, we'll receive. If we seek, we'll find. If we knock, the door will be opened. I'm not sure how God will give you "the things God has prepared for those who love him," but I'm convinced He'll find a way.

God has used all kinds of methods to teach me about my identity. He speaks through His Word, often illuminating a passage I've read a hundred times, but I see it in a new way. He has given me visions and dreams that have deepened my understanding of His purpose for me. As I've prayed, God has broken into my consciousness to give me assurance and direction. And He has confirmed His revelation through people. I've had many significant mentors, teachers, and friends, but God has given me three men as my spiritual fathers. Their voices are calm, clear, and powerful. More than any others, God has used them to deepen my understanding of who I am, challenge me to be all God wants me to be, and rest in God's greatness and grace. I'll introduce them to you in this book. I hope the perspectives I've gained from them will transfer to you as you see how they have affirmed my God-given identity.

I want to make a bold statement: I believe God's design for each of us is to bring spiritual fathers and mothers into our lives. The concept of spiritual parenting is powerful. God could have saved us and made us His slaves or employees, but He adopted us as His sons and daughters, and He has promised that we will share in Christ's inheritance. We're in! And to make this truth sink it, He gives us people to serve as His voice, His hands, and His arms as models of His presence in our lives.

Our role is to look for these people and be receptive when God reveals them. The last promise and warning in the Old Testament is about the importance

> **I want to make a bold statement: I believe God's design for each of us is to bring spiritual fathers and mothers into our lives.**

of our relationship with parents (and spiritual parents). Through Malachi, God spoke:

"See, I will send the prophet Elijah to you before that great and dreadful day of the Lord comes. He will turn the hearts of the parents to their children, and the hearts of the children to their parents; or else I will come and strike the land with total destruction." —Malachi 4:5-6

I believe God is working on both sides of these connections: I see Christian leaders with a heart to invest in the growth of young men and women, and I see young people turning to mature, gifted, loving leaders for guidance. I don't think I'm saying too much when I say that I believe this is the hope of the church. Great programs, big buildings, and grand visions are fine, but they only matter when they're led by people who have been spiritually parented—nurtured, affirmed, corrected, and challenged—in loving relationships.

MY HOPE FOR YOU

As I began writing this book, a friend asked me who it's for. I thought for a minute and then told him, "I think it's for anyone who wants his life to count but lacks confidence, people who desperately want all of God and who desperately want God to have all of them. They're willing to bring all their talents and all their hopes, as well as all their hurts and hang-ups. They have big dreams, but they also have big fears. God has given them a desire to follow Him and discover what He has called them to be and do. They have more confidence in God than in who they are in Him. They know He's wise and great and loving, but when they look in the mirror, they see doubt instead of courage. They may be students or grandparents. They may be pastors or plumbers. They may be city officials or people who just came to our country. This book is for anyone who is haunted by the fear that they might let God down—those who have faith in God but struggle to have faith in who they are in God.

In this book, I'm inviting you into my story. In essence, it's my auto-biography, and like any good story, you'll see plenty of tragic flaws, plot twists, and emerging heroes. At various times in my life, I've been a mess. I've had misguided motives, a limited vision, and self-absorbed goals. The hero of this story certainly isn't me. First and foremost, the hero is Jesus, who loves me, rescued me, and by His grace, is changing me from the inside out. But there are also other heroes. I'll share how God used my three spiritual fathers (my dad, John Maxwell, and Sam Chand) to help me discover my identity. The principles they taught me apply far more widely than to just me. If you open your heart to their words, they can help you discover your identity as well. Their words are truth and life. I hope you'll hear them speaking to you, too.

At the end of the introduction and every chapter, you'll find some questions designed to stimulate personal reflection, and perhaps, dis-cussion with your spouse, your close friends, your mentor, or your counselor. The goal isn't to finish them as quickly as possible. Take your time. Think, pray, and consider how events and people have shaped your identity, your drives, and your fears.

Chapter 1

The Dream

My father, Tom Wilson, was a powerfully positive voice in my life until the day he passed away. When I was growing up, he was my hero. I was sure he was the smartest person on the planet, and he worked harder than anyone I knew. He taught me to pray, he planted the Word in my heart, and he demonstrated a huge heart of compassion for everyone who came across his path. He spent time with me, played games with me, and found creative ways to communicate, *I love you*, and *You're special.* For him, every moment was an opportunity to teach me something. He had confidence that God was going to use me, and he believed my future was even better than his. I have no idea how many times he told me, "Son, I'll give you everything I have, but it's up to you to take it from there."

In the summer after I graduated from high school, when I was seventeen, I went on a stateside mission trip with our youth group. In one of the evening services, I walked off to the side to pray. I sensed God ask, *Are you ready to give everything you are to Me?*

"Yes, Lord," I replied. "I love You. You know I'm ready."

I felt Him say, *I want to know if you're ready to be completely devoted to Me because I'm ready to use you now and in a big way.*

Immediately, I knew this was a pivotal moment in my life, a "line in the sand" that demanded a decision. I responded, "Of course. I'm Yours."

This means you'll look to Me for where you go to school, who you'll marry, where you'll serve, how you'll serve, how you'll respond to opportunities and heartaches . . . everything. At this point, you're saved, but you're not fully surrendered. That's what I'm asking: will you fully surrender every aspect of your life to Me?

I prayed at the altar for two hours. Tears streamed down my face. I pleaded, "God, I'll go anywhere and do anything for You. Just don't skip over me! Please be patient with me!"

I had no idea what all this meant, but I was sure it was a turning point in my life. Four days after I got home from the missions trip, my dad told me, "Our youth pastor has resigned. Son, would you lead until we can find someone to replace him?"

I began to stammer my hesitation, but Dad interrupted, "I know these are your peers, and I'm asking you to lead them. Son, I wouldn't ask you to do this if I didn't think you could do it. I see God's hand on you."

Again, I began my speech that I wasn't ready, but Dad just shook his head and told me, "We'll pay you $100 a week. You can line up people to speak each week. You can plan the activities and lead them. I'm sure you'll do a great job."

"Okay, I'll do my best." End of conversation.

For the first few weeks, I asked different people to speak to the youth group. Then, one evening a guy cancelled at the last minute, and I had no one else to turn to. It was up to me to share that night. I prayed and asked God, "What am I supposed to say? I don't know how to preach."

I sensed God tell me, *Son, just get up and tell them what I've been telling you each morning as you spend time with Me.*

What a great plan for preaching—just get up and tell people what God's been telling you. After I spoke that night, I cancelled the other speakers. I knew I was born for this!

I'd never had any classes on hermeneutics or preaching. Each week, I got up and spoke on whatever I'd learned in my devotional time during the previous week. Over the next six months, the size of our youth group tripled, and a lot of kids got saved. The church was paying me only $100 a week, so my dad asked, "Scott, are you ready to go full time?" I've never looked back.

My dad poured himself into me, and he believed in me when there was no visible reason to have that level of confidence in me. That's what good dads do. They see you, not for who you are, but for the person you are becoming. And they call that greatness out in you.

Two years after taking the youth pastor position full time, Dad walked in and announced, "Son, God has shown me that He has called us to Dallas."

I couldn't believe it. Our church was thriving. Why in the world would we leave something so good to go where we didn't know anybody? Didn't the people of Austin need Jesus every bit as much as those in Dallas? When I voiced my concerns, Dad told me, "Just pray about it. I've prayed about it, and God has been

> **They see you, not for who you are, but for the person you are becoming. And they call that greatness out in you.**

very clear. He'll be clear with you, too." He let that sink in, and then he told me, "The board at the church in Dallas asked if they could interview you as the new youth pastor."

My head was spinning. I told him, "I, uh, sure. If that's where you're going. . . ."

We moved to the Oak Cliff community of Dallas. Dad was challenged and inspired to take this new role as the pastor. The board must have decided it was a package deal because they hired me as the youth pastor. I felt like a fish out of water—insecure, alone, and intimidated. I had left a church where I'd known every student and had gone to school with many of them, but now I had to get to know people, uncover the teenage alliances that are in every youth group, and earn credibility. I was sure people saw me as the tagalong pastor's kid. To compensate for my shaky identity, I was determined to win respect by being a powerful, decisive leader. Richie Brown had been leading the youth group before I arrived. I was smart enough to realize I needed his friendship if I was ever going to make it with the students, and he became a big resource for me. It was one of my only smart moves in those early months in Dallas.

A year or two later, I felt better about my role in the church. We were reaching kids, leading many to Christ, and seeing growth, but I wasn't satisfied. I was sure God was calling me to do great things. I dreamed of growing a great church where people who were far from God could be saved and grow to be dynamic disciples. The problem was that I didn't have a strategy to fulfill the dream.

MY DAD'S ADVICE

Dad told our staff team that he was taking us to Phoenix to a conference at Tommy Barnett's church. At the time, Pastor Barnett was already a legend. He had built one of the biggest churches in the country, with over fifty ministries for every conceivable group of people, from motorcycle gangs to people with physical challenges, from care for unwed moms to those struggling with addiction. God was doing incredible things there, and I was excited to go.

In his first message, Pastor Barnett explained his "secret" to church growth: "God gave me a vision that we should be a soul-winning church." Man, I was already on board with whatever he was going to say! He continued, "For us, it's simple. Our strategy is to 'Find a need and fill it. Find a hurt and heal it.'"

In that moment, I had two powerful but conflicting emotions. I was inspired by Pastor Barnett's clear vision and plan, but I was frustrated that God hadn't given me a vision statement like that. I sat in the audience fuming.

After the message, I went to the altar. I prayed, *God, why are You holding out on me? You've called me to greatness, but I'm stuck! Why haven't You given me a statement like You gave Pastor Barnett?* I was sure I was only one cool phrase away from greatness.

I don't know how long I was at the altar. I poured my heart out to God. I pleaded with Him to speak to me, to give me what I needed to do great things for Him. Suddenly, I felt a touch on my shoulder. Was it the Holy Spirit answering my prayers? Was I about to hear God's clear, bold voice? The words came: "Son, I appreciate that you're praying, but we're all in the van. Hurry up. We're getting hungry." It wasn't my heavenly Father talking; it was my "hungry" father telling me it was time to go. When we got outside, the others in the van had already left for the restaurant. Dad and I got in the rental car, and he started driving.

After only a few minutes, he looked over at me and asked, "Scott, why are you so angry?"

I guess I felt safe being completely honest with him. I erupted, "Dad, I'm so frustrated! I've been asking God to give me a big vision like He gave Pastor Barnett, but nothing's happening!"

Dad didn't miss a beat. He calmly asked, "Son, what has God already told you to do?"

I couldn't believe it. Dad wasn't on my side at all. I growled, "I don't know. He hasn't told me anything."

Again, with no heightened emotions, Dad pulled the car over, looked at me, and said, "Son, He's already told you what to do."

Now I was getting really upset. I shook my head and insisted, "No, He hasn't!"

Dad asked, "How about the Great Commandment to love God and love people?"

He wasn't helping. I barked back, "He's called everybody to do that! I want Him to give me something bigger, better, and more specific!"

Dad looked over and smiled. He told me, "Son, that's it. That's what He has called you to do. I promise you: if you're faithful to love God with all your heart, mind, and strength, and you're faithful to love people like He loves them, He'll give you the details when you need them. If you're not willing to do what He has already called you to do, why would He give you more specific directions and a bigger calling?"

I've never forgotten his wise advice. And I've never forgotten the look of kindness on his face when he spoke those words. Something shifted inside me at that moment—it wasn't a complete resolution of my frustration, but it was a big step in the right direction. I could trust

God and His process of leading me. He's not hiding from me, and He's not playing games with me.

Today I look back on those moments and wonder, *What was I thinking? How could I imagine God would give me, still just a kid, a vision comparable to one He gave Tommy Barnett, who had been a gifted leader for more than thirty years at the time?* I guess that's the tendency of youth—to want to skip process, but God loved me too much to let me skip the process that would help me to not just be successful in ministry, but to become the man He wanted me to be.

> **I could trust God and His process of leading me. He's not hiding from me, and He's not playing games with me.**

SHOULDERS

A few months later, back in Dallas, I had a dream. It's as vivid today as it was thirty years ago. I was on a stage preaching to a vast audience at an outdoor crusade. Tens of thousands of people listened to me tell them about Jesus. People streamed forward to be saved, and others were healed from all kinds of sickness and infirmities. God's Spirit was moving powerfully. I was standing on a platform behind a large wooden podium, so people could only see me from the chest up. In the dream, I looked down and saw a large hole in the platform under me. My father was standing in the hole, and I was standing on his shoulders. He was holding my ankles, so I didn't slip and fall. His eyes were closed. He was praying, and tears streamed down his cheeks.

In the dream, I sensed the Lord tell me, *Everybody thinks you're standing on a platform you built for yourself, but in reality, you're standing on the shoulders of your father.*

Some dreams need an interpretation; not this one—it was crystal clear. When I woke up, I called my dad and thanked him for being the foundation of my life and encouraging me to serve God.

I told God that from that day forward, I was committed to be the shoulders others could stand on. Instead of being devoted to "platform ministry," I was devoted to "shoulder ministry." I had been consumed with my own success, but on that day, my focus shifted to others' success.

The dream, the vision, the commitment isn't just about me, and it's not just about pastors. It's the calling for everyone who is connected to the next generation: mothers, fathers, grandparents, uncles, aunts, teachers, coaches, mentors, bosses, and spiritual leaders of all kinds. All of us can make a solemn commitment to be the shoulders young people can stand on. My dad had told me, "Son, I'll give you everything I have, and you need to take it from there." That's what I'm saying to the people who stand on my shoulders: "I'll give you everything I have, and it's up to you to take what I give you and multiply it in the lives of more people." I give them the wealth of the spiritual inheritance my dad has entrusted to me, so they can begin with plenty of resources to honor God with their whole hearts.

This is what I was made for. I had been frustrated only months before because God hadn't given me a bold, clear calling. Now He had.

Actually, this is the legacy Jesus promised. On the night before His arrest, He spent a long time with His disciples to prepare them for His departure. In response to Philip's doubts, Jesus explained that He was standing on the Father's shoulders:

> *"Don't you know me, Philip, even after I have been among you such*
> *a long time? Anyone who has seen me has seen the Father. How*
> *can you say, 'Show us the Father'? Don't you believe that I am in*
> *the Father, and that the Father is in me? The words I say to you I*
> *do not speak on my own authority. Rather, it is the Father, living in*
> *me, who is doing his work. Believe me when I say that I am in the*
> *Father and the Father is in me; or at least believe on the evidence*
> *of the works themselves." —John 14:9-11*

But that's not the end of things. Jesus then explained that the discipl
were going to stand on His shoulders, and stunningly, do more than F
did! Their minds must have been spinning when He told them,

> *"Very truly I tell you, whoever believes in me will do the works I*
> *have been doing, and they will do even greater things than these,*
> *because I am going to the Father. And I will do whatever you ask in*
> *my name, so that the Father may be glorified in the Son. You may*
> *ask me for anything in my name, and I will do it." —John 14:12-1*

Jesus' vision for those who follow Him is to do bigger and be
things—greater in every way—than He did. How? By standing on
shoulders. There, we experience love, forgiveness, security, and po
And if we grasp His invitation, "Follow Me," we'll follow His exar
and invite people to stand on our shoulders. When generation
generation stands on their predecessors' shoulders, the kingdo
God will grow exponentially. That's my dad's impact on me, and
God's vision for me to give everything I am and everything I ha
the people standing on my shoulders.

This is the vision God gave me in the dream when I was twenty
old, and it's the vision that will propel me until the day I die.

THE DEAL

The morning after I woke up from the dream, I made a deal w
I told Him, "I'll devote my life to raise up as many spiritual so⌐
daughters as I can, including my own three sons, so the next generat⌐
will be stronger than ours. Someday, I expect my dad to step down an⌐
pass the church to me, and someday, I'll step down and pass the church
to someone else. I trust You to choose and place people, including my
successor, any way You choose. I'll concentrate on loving all the ones
You bring to me. I'll equip them, support them, and give them everything I've got. Where they serve is up to You."

I was completely convinced that the impact of my life wasn't going
to be what I did on the platform, but what I did under the platform
This is my commitment with my sons, with my grandchildren, with the
pastors God has given me to coach, and with the people in our church.

IN PRACTICE

From the day I woke up from the dream, I knew God was leading me to
implement programs and systems to equip the people who would stand
on my shoulders. We'd heard about some churches that had created a
"Master's Commission" for young men and women who were taking
a gap year out of college for an intense discipleship program. These
young people learn how to study the Scriptures, how to pray, and how
to discover God's call for their lives. I told my dad, "I'd like to do this
at our church."

He replied, "Then go ahead."

I probably laughed when I said, "But I don't have a clue how to do it."

"You'll figure it out," was his confident answer.

And we did. The Oaks School of Leadership began, and it has equipped more than five hundred young adults. It is now a fully accredited college program.

At the time we launched our School of Leadership, I knew I had to keep growing to stay ahead of our students. Dave Dawson at Dallas Theological Seminary had a two-year course called "Equipping the Saints." The classes taught students how to multiply themselves into the next generation and the next. It was exactly what I was looking for to equip me to do what God had called me to do. I enlisted fifty people from our youth group to join me in taking it. It was a challenging course, but I finished in one year.

Our church saw the very real impact of our "shoulder ministry." Within a few years, Dad hired three people who had been through our training, and they became vital members of our growing team.

I started a monthly training for youth pastors in the Dallas area. We called it Inside Out. Each month, I spoke, and I invited a guest speaker to talk about reaching kids, relating to the culture, and growing youth ministries.

One day, my dad called me into his office. He said, "Son, you've learned everything I can teach you. Now I want to introduce you to someone who can take you to the next step in your development. It's John Maxwell." He handed me a cassette tape and told me, "Listen to this. It'll inspire you and give you ideas about how to make your ministry excel." Then he walked

Then he walked over to a huge cabinet and opened the doors. There were hundreds of cassette tapes!

over to a huge cabinet and opened the doors. There were hundreds of cassette tapes!

I laughed and said, "Dad, you've been holding out on me!"

"I didn't know you'd be interested," he said with a smile.

"Yeah," I told him. "I'm interested."

To say I devoured Maxwell's messages isn't much of an overstatement. Each Monday, Dad gave me a stack of five cassettes. The drive to the church was about twenty minutes each way, so I could listen to one each day. Out of the five, I picked one that was particularly meaningful. I listened to it again to get the points and the flow of thought in my mind. Then, I listened a third time to memorize it. Our youth group leadership team met on Sunday afternoons before the students arrived, and I taught John's message to our leaders. They thought I was brilliant!

This was the pattern of my drives, my training, my messages, and my life for three years. I was utterly captivated by John's insights and his heart. It's difficult to overestimate the impact he had on me during those years. My dad could have introduced me earlier to his extensive library of John Maxwell cassettes, but the Lord led him to open the cabinet at just the right time. After the first one, I was all in.

CLEARING AWAY THE FOG

When I look back on my frustration that day when Tommy Barnett shared the secret of his success, I have more understanding about the condition of my heart. It's easy for our purpose to be a bit misguided—or maybe a lot misguided. I assumed my passion for greatness was in perfect alignment with God's design, but in hindsight, I can see that it was far too much about me and not enough about God. I wanted to prove myself, to be great in the eyes of people I respect, to be noticed and applauded.

Did I want to honor God? Sure, but I'm afraid I got ways and means mixed up. Honoring God was a means to my end of personal success—not completely, but more than is healthy, good, and right. The dream was a major course correction. My purpose was no longer to establish my glory, but God's. It was no longer about my success, but my commitment to serve the people God put in my life, so they'd be successful. All of us have mixed motives. The question is how we respond when the Holy Spirit shines a light on them.

The dream corrected my vision, refocused my compelling purpose, and reoriented my heart. In an incredibly powerful way, the Spirit of God demonstrated the impact my dad had on me by letting me stand on his shoulders, and I knew—in the depths of my soul—that God was calling me to continue and expand his legacy by letting people stand on my shoulders.

Chapter 2

Crushed and Rebuilt

In my early twenties, I was determined to be one of the greatest leaders in the world. I was willing to go anywhere, do anything, and pay any price. I imagined people would one day think of me like I thought of John Maxwell—famous, respected, powerful, and sought after. Like he did, I wanted to have an impact on world leaders, travel the world to meet with national officials and church leaders, and have an open door to the halls of power in the United States. Basically, I wanted to be the next John Maxwell. (That's not asking too much, is it?)

During those years, I was flooding my mind and heart with John's messages on cassette. I signed up to get his monthly leadership CDs, and I began using the recently released ones for my messages to our youth leaders. Like I'd done before, I picked one I especially liked, listened three times, and by the third time, I had not only his words, but his intonations.

A friend of mine, Joe Centineo, was a youth pastor in the Dallas Metroplex. I had met Joe on a youth pastors' retreat with Leadership Network. He was an amazing youth pastor. After getting to know him,

31

I discovered that he had been the youth pastor at Skyline Church with John Maxwell. I asked him what it was like to work with John.

Joe told story after story, and I couldn't get enough.

One day, Joe called to tell me John was coming to Dallas to speak. I told him, "I don't want to be presumptuous, but I want to meet him to tell him how much his teaching has meant to me."

"That's cool," Joe nodded.

But I wanted more than that. I told him, "I want to tell him I want to be a great leader, and ask him for any advice he'd give me."

"Very cool."

But I didn't tell Joe that I had imagined that John would look me in the eyes and say, "Oh, Scott! I've been looking for a young man just like you. I want you on my team. I'm convinced God is going to use you in amazing ways, and I want you to be a part of it all!"

No, I didn't say that, but I was sure thinking it.

Joe had an idea. He said, "Hey, here's what you need to do. Put a $100 bill in an envelope and write a note telling him you want thirty minutes with him."

"Don't you think that would be a bit . . . weird?"

"Heck, no!" Joe was excited about it. "That's exactly what he did when he got started. He put $100 bills in envelopes and gave them to the pastors of the ten largest churches in America. You can do it, too! He'll recognize himself in it, and you'll make an instant connection!"

I was stoked! Before the conference, I scrounged up $100, wrote a note, and put them in an envelope. That morning, Jenni and I prayed together. She knew how important this was to me. As I walked out the door, I put the envelope in my pocket. I was ready.

The event was at Prestonwood Baptist Church, which at the time had a sanctuary that held about three thousand people. I arrived early (really early), so I could get a seat on the front row . . . right in the middle, so John couldn't miss me. Soon, the room was packed. I was convinced that some kind of celestial light would shine on me, and John would supernaturally recognize my incredible potential. He might even stop his message and come down to publicly tap me as his new partner and successor.

I knew John used a yellow legal pad for his notes, so I brought one with me. When he started speaking, I frantically wrote every key line he said. And to punctuate each one, I audibly said, "Wow!" and nodded my head with awe. When he said something funny, I slapped my leg, threw my head back, laughed uproariously, and said to the person next to me, "Did you hear that?" (Did I think he was deaf?) He ended his message with a heart-wrenching story that brought tears to everyone's eyes, including John's. He prayed a powerful prayer for God's blessings over all of us. After he said, "Amen," he explained, "Thank you so much for being here today. Unfortunately, I have to run out and catch a plane, so I don't have time to stay around to talk with you. God bless you." And he started walking off the platform.

An abrupt departure wasn't in my plans at all. It was obviously a terrible time to try to talk to him, but in my mind, it was now or never. As he was hurrying away, I intercepted him. "Dr. Maxwell, I'm Scott Wilson, a youth pastor here in Dallas. I've listened to every one of your cassettes and CDs, and I've read all of your books. Thank you so much for all of your teaching. I'm a huge fan. I've learned so much from you, and I sense that someday I'm going to do what you do. Do you have any advice for me?"

He wiped the remaining tear from his cheek. Then he looked me in the eye and took a deep breath. This was it. This is what I'd been dreaming of! He put his hand on my shoulder and said in his low, baritone voice, "Son, you don't even know what you're asking." He abruptly turned and walked out the door.

The envelope was still in my pocket, and my heart was on the floor.

I was crushed.

I hoped nobody had overheard our brief conversation. I was humiliated enough without people snickering and pointing at me.

> **He put his hand on my shoulder and said . . . "Son, you don't even know what you're asking."**

When I got home and opened the front door, Jenni was excited and asked, "How did it go? What happened?"

I shrugged, "Nothing."

It was obvious from the look on her face that I needed to explain a bit more, so I told her, "There wasn't time to talk to him. He had to catch a flight." She could tell my disappointment was caused by more than inconvenience, but to her credit, she didn't probe.

AND GOD SHOWED UP

I went into our bedroom and closed the door. I got on my knees and poured out my heart in prayer: "God, what just happened? Why did he treat me like that? I know You've called me to be a leader, and he would be the perfect mentor for me. It could have worked out so well!"

At that moment, I sensed the Lord tell me, *Son, why are you looking to John Maxwell as your source? He didn't make you. I did. He didn't save you. I did. He's not the one who is going to make you the leader I want you to be. I am. I know what I've put into you, and I know how to develop those skills, so you can use them to do great things.* After a minute or two, He continued, *When are you going to trust Me? When are you going to stop trying to make things happen in your timing and in your way? I haven't called you to be the next John Maxwell. I've called you to be the first Scott Wilson.*

My heavenly Father broke through my despair and my shattered dreams to say, "You need to trust in My plan. You need to trust in My timing. I'm the Lord. Do you think I'm going to delegate the responsibility to shape you to John? Trust Me even when your hopes are dashed. Trust Me when you're disappointed, when you go through hard times, when things aren't moving as fast as you'd like. Trust Me like Jesus trusted Me."

The Lord graciously reminded me of a scene on the night Jesus was betrayed. Earlier that evening, Jesus had dinner with the disciples. He had told them many times that He was going to be betrayed into the hands of sinful men, falsely accused, and executed. He knew this was the night spiritual darkness would fall—one of them was going to hand Him over to the Jewish leaders. The Lord of Life would be mocked, falsely accused, wrongly convicted, tortured, and killed.

If anyone deserved understanding and compassion at that moment, it was Jesus. Instead, the disciples bickered about who among them would be the greatest in the new kingdom. (Hmmm. That sounded vaguely familiar.)

If I'd been Jesus, I would have been so angry with them! How could they be so self-centered, so callous, so insensitive? I would have yelled, "You don't get it. I'm about to die on a cross for the sins of all mankind, and you guys are arguing about who's going to be the greatest? Come on!" But that's not what happened.

John sets the scene for us: "It was just before the Passover Festival. Jesus knew that the hour had come for him to leave this world and go to the Father. Having loved his own who were in the world, he loved them to the end" (John 13:1). In John's gospel, "the hour" always refers to Jesus' death. It was time. John said that He "loved them to the end." This could mean that He loved them to the end of His earthly life, but I think it means He loved them to the *nth* degree, the deepest, highest, longest, and widest extent of love. What does this love look like? The disciples were put in charge of preparing for the meal, but they had forgotten to have a servant wash everyone's feet, which was the custom when anyone entered a home, especially for an important dinner. But there was a different kind of Servant in the room. "[Jesus] got up from the meal, took off his outer clothing, and wrapped a towel around his waist. After that, he poured water into a basin and began to wash his disciples' feet, drying them with the towel that was wrapped around him" (vv. 4-5).

As I prayed in the bedroom and reflected on this scene, I sensed the Father say, *Look at this event and think about what Jesus knew.* It says it right there in the passage: Jesus knew it was time for Him to go to the cross to be the perfect sacrifice to pay for our sins. In that moment of the greatest pressure anyone has ever endured, Jesus knew the Father was in complete control, He knew the Father had sent Him, and He knew the Father would empower Him to fulfill His purpose. None of what was happening was a surprise to God. Nothing had fallen out of His strong and loving hands.

When I had walked out of our house that morning, I was sure God wanted to open the door for me to have a relationship with John Max well. John's quick dismissal wasn't just a disappointment; it was my failure to fulfill what I believed was God's calling to be a valued member of John's team.

I'm sure the reason I felt so devastated was that John's messages on cassettes and CDs were equipping me to do exactly what God had called me to do: disciple people, so they become fully devoted followers of Christ. And I was seeing amazing results.

> **None of what was happening was a surprise to God. Nothing had fallen out of His strong and loving hands.**

As I taught our leaders and our students what I was learning from John, people were being saved, hurts were being healed, and lives were turned around. It was electric! John was pouring himself into me (electronically), and I was pouring myself into every person around me. Surely, surely, God would want John and me to have a closer relationship. But the answer—God's answer that came from John's lips—was a resounding, "No!"

I wasn't upset with John. It wasn't his fault that his schedule didn't allow him to meet with me, and it had become abundantly clear that I was expecting way too much of him when I parked myself in the middle of the front row. I was more upset with God for not coming through like I expected.

In that moment in the bedroom, I knew that I couldn't act like Jesus unless I learned to think like Jesus. I felt deeply relieved that God was speaking to me, but I also felt challenged to reorient my perspective at the deepest level of my heart. Could I trust that God was still in control even though my plans didn't work out? Could I trust that God had sent me into ministry, and He would shape me and prepare me to do exactly what He called me to do?

Jesus knew the Father's purposes would be fulfilled, whether He spoke to thousands on a hillside in Galilee or He was being whipped, beaten, and murdered on a Roman cross. Could I believe that the Father's purposes in my life would be fulfilled when my plans didn't work out the way I expected? In His timing and in His way, God promised to prepare me to be who He wants me to be, go where He wants me to go, and do what He wants me to do. That's what I needed to know. That's what I needed to believe.

Did I believe these truths before that day? Yes, I could articulate the theology of divine sovereignty. I could explain how God planned for Joseph to be betrayed by his brothers and spend long years in prison in Egypt, so he would be in the right place at the right time to save that part of the world—including his father and brothers—from starvation. I had taught our youth leaders the principles of discipleship and how God prepares each of us to fulfill His calling. But at a fundamental level, I still wanted my plans more than God's plans, I wanted my fame more than His fame, and I wanted to control the process instead of trusting in His timing. My realization was a call to repentance. My deep disappointment had become a crucial turning point in my walk with God.

In almost three decades since that moment, I've had plenty of opportunities to think like Jesus, so I could act more like Jesus. Countless times, things haven't gone the way I expected, and I've had to go back to these truths: God is in control, I'm not. God has sent me, but

His path inevitably winds through darkness, heartache, and setbacks. And I can trust that God will empower me to do what He has called me to do—including facing hard times with patience and serving those who seem ungrateful. He has given me the gifts and experiences I need to fulfill His calling, and a big part of this calling is the ability to lead people with grace and strength in the middle of difficulties.

Jesus was convinced of these truths in the core of His being. Am I? Are you?

My dad's words echoed in my heart: *Son, just love God with all your heart and love people. If you do that, God will open plenty of doors for you.*

DEATH OF A DREAM

Dreamers are vulnerable. People with high hopes can have those hopes dashed, and they can fall hard. I know. I'm one of them. Some people cope with the risk of being hurt by shattered dreams by not having any, or making them so small that they can control the outcome. That's not me, and it's probably not you. In my own experience, and as I've talked with hundreds of leaders over the years, I've noticed a cycle that often happens: big dreams are followed by crystallizing hopes, then hints of trouble and failure, the death of the dream, burial and grief.

In the beginning, we were so sure. That's why it hurts so

> **Dreamers are vulnerable. People with high hopes can have those hopes dashed, and they can fall hard. I know. I'm one of them.**

bad. Some authors describe the sense of God's abandonment as "the dark night of the soul." It's awful. God seems to have vanished, and our prayers feel empty. God sometimes uses these intense times of pain as seasons of reorientation—to His heart, His purposes, and His timing. Thankfully, my season was only a few hours in the bedroom, but that's not always the case. It's not even usually the case. Some people experience unsettling grief for a long time. I think God's attitude is, "Whatever it takes to reorient you to My plans, My timing, and My heart, I'll do it. And I'm not in a hurry."

The Christian message is that Jesus didn't stay in the grave. Three days later, He was resurrected. That, too, is part of our stories when our dreams die. Sometimes, God raises up our initial dream and fulfills it, but more often, He makes it far better than it would have been. No, we don't have that faith when we're in the pit of despair when our dream's corpse is on the floor, but later, maybe much later, God will give us something that's even more wonderful, has a greater impact, and is even more fulfilling.

My dream died when John's hand left my shoulder, and he turned to walk out the door. A few hours later in my bedroom, God began the process of reorienting me. It was humbling but not humiliating. God didn't smash me like a bug . . . probably like I deserved. He was wonderfully present, wonderfully gracious, and wonderfully clear in showing me a path forward. I had been crushed, but the rebuilding process had already begun.

Can you and I trust that God, the sovereign King of the universe, is in control of all things—that He knows far more than we do, has far higher purposes than ours, and loves us more than we can know? Can we trust that God has sent us to fulfill His calling, in the same way He sent Jesus, and His path inevitably includes temptation, opposition, and suffering, as we choose to serve even ungrateful people?

Chapter 3

Breaking the Orphan Mindset

Several years after the John Maxwell debacle, I attended another conference where he spoke. I had just become the co-pastor with my dad, and we were very interested in the topic: "Breaking the 1000 Barrier." Another speaker at the event who really impressed me was Gerald Brooks. I didn't know that he lived just up the road in Plano, Texas. He was amazing. When I found out he was hosting a staffing seminar, I signed up. I met him at the seminar, and during the next two years, we developed a close friendship.

Gerald was on John Maxwell's board for his missions organization called EQUIP. One day he called me and said, "Scott, the EQUIP board is meeting for a two-day training with John in Atlanta in a few weeks, and he said we could each invite one person to join us. Would you like to go with me?"

It didn't take me long to respond. I blurted out, "Absolutely!"

As soon as I hung up the phone, I thought, *This is incredible! I'm going to spend time with John in a group of forty of the sharpest leaders on the planet, and I get to hang out with Gerald, who is a genius!* It had been ten years since Prestonwood, and thankfully, I had grown a lot. This time I wasn't going to try to be seen or noticed. I just wanted to learn.

We flew to Atlanta the night before the training began. The next morning, Gerald and I arrived at John's office. The room was set up in a big circle. John walked in and went around the room shaking people's hands as board members introduced him to each of the twenty guests. I was the kid in the group, and I was really excited. When he finished greeting everyone, we all found a seat. It just so happened that the only empty seat was next to me. John came over and sat down.

He began, "Hi. I'm John. I'm your friend. Thank you for coming. I'm going to give you a behind-the-scenes preview of my new book on the pain of being a leader. My publisher has given permission for me to give you copies of the manuscript, and you'll get a copy today. You know what it feels like to go through pain and endure hardship, or you wouldn't be the successful leaders you are. You are the pastors of great churches. When people look at you, they see your incredible gifts and your exemplary leadership skills. They see people being saved, and they know how God is using you to change individuals and families. They hear how you're having an impact across the country and around the world. They see the anointing on you, and they think to themselves, *Wow, I want to be like him!*

But they don't have a chance to look behind the curtain to see the hours you agonize with people whose lives are falling apart, with parents whose child has died, with your board members who doubt you'll meet budget this month, with the wife whose husband was killed in an accident, with your own wife and kids who struggle to cope with the pressures on them because of your role. They don't know the pain you feel so intensely." He paused, and then said, "They don't have any idea what it takes to be the kind of leader you are."

John didn't miss a beat. "I remember speaking at a conference at Prestonwood Baptist Church in Dallas about ten years ago. After I spoke, a young man who had been sitting on the front row came up to me and said, 'Dr. Maxwell, I want to be like you when I grow up.' The kid was so eager and excited, but he didn't know the price tag attached to his request. He craved a platform and the applause of men, but he didn't understand what it would cost. I patted him on the shoulder, and said, 'Young man, you don't even know what you're asking.'"

At that moment, I wished I'd told Gerald that I had a root canal scheduled for the day of this meeting, so I couldn't go with him. I wished I could disintegrate on the spot, evaporate and vanish, turn the clock back ten years, and have a flat tire on the way to Prestonwood. Anything!

I had become a John Maxwell illustration.

John had no idea the kid who came up to him that day was sitting right next to him, and I certainly wasn't going to tell him. I'm not sure I breathed the rest of the day. I didn't hear another word in the meetings because the only thing I could think about was the irony—no, the absurdity—of John telling this story with me sitting next to him.

When I got back to my hotel room that night, it was

> **At that moment, I wished I'd told Gerald that I had a root canal scheduled for the day of this meeting, so I couldn't go with him.**

a replay of my prayer in the bedroom a decade before. I prayed, "God, John had no idea, but You did. Why did You let me come? Why did You have him sit next to me? Of the thousands and thousands of stories he could have told, why did he tell that one?" I was sure it wasn't a coincidence. This was every bit as much of a "God moment" as it had been in my bedroom years earlier.

The Lord again reminded me of a passage of scripture, but this time in Matthew 20:20-23. The mother of James and John had obviously been dreaming of the future with her sons. They had visions of power, authority, and prestige. She came to Jesus with her boys and knelt down in front of Him. She requested, "Grant that one of these two sons of mine may sit at your right and the other at your left in your kingdom."

Jesus replied, not to her, but to the sons, "You don't know what you are asking."

I froze when I read it. There it was again!

Then He asked them, "Can you drink the cup I am going to drink?"

"We can," they answered.

Jesus told them, "You will indeed drink from my cup, but to sit at my right or left is not for me to grant. These places belong to those for whom they have been prepared by my Father."

In the Bible, "the cup" may represent God's blessing, but more often, it represents His suffering. It's the pain John was talking about earlier in the day. Leaders have to be willing to drink the cup of suffering and obedience if they want to be used by God. If James and John were committed to follow Jesus, they would have to pay a steep price. They would suffer like He was to suffer, they would be mocked like He was mocked, and they would be abandoned like He was abandoned by all but one disciple, His mother, and a few faithful women. But Jesus also told them that there were no guarantees about any place of prominence in the kingdom. Seats are assigned by the Father, not demanded or chosen by us. Jesus was telling James and John that if they paid the price only to achieve personal fame and power, it was useless. But if they paid the price of suffering to bring God glory, they wouldn't care what seats of honor He gave them.

Jesus was willing to do whatever the Father told Him to do, and that's what He was asking from the two brothers: to do whatever He told them to do—without any strings attached.

As I read this passage, the Father spoke to me: *I have a seat for you, and it has your name on it. No one can take it from you; no one can steal it. I'm preparing you for it. Stop trying to push and shove to make things happen. Your seat is My choice, not yours. I can put you in any seat I choose in any room, next to any person, for any purpose, and today, I chose the seat for you next to John. It wasn't because you maneuvered yourself into that seat, and it wasn't an accident. I did it on purpose. Trust Me. Trust My process. Trust My timing. Don't strive to be great. Be content with My calling and My process. Greatness isn't your goal. Your goal is to follow Me, love Me with all your heart, listen to Me, and obey Me. Greatness is the outcome, and it's up to Me.*

The Lord was assuring me, *You're not alone. You're never alone. I love you, and I'm with you.*

I had mistakenly equated contentment and complacency. All of my heroes are zealous, go-for-broke kinds of people, not those who are satisfied with small dreams.

> **I discovered that contentment is the byproduct of certainty.**

Contentment seemed too passive, too lame, too ordinary. But I was wrong. I discovered that contentment is the byproduct of certainty. When we know we're in the middle of God's will, when we're convinced there's nothing we can do to lose His affection, and when we're sure God will lead us, our level of worry can recede without diminishing our passion for God and His purposes. We know we're right where God wants us to be, trusting in His process. We're not forcing anything, and we're not timid and hesitating.

Those who walk closely with God have a beautiful blend of zeal and contentment. Their drive isn't clouded by comparison or the fear of not measuring up. They can give it all they've got and trust that God will do what only He can do. That's the kind of contentment I crave. That's the kind of contentment only God can give.

ALONE AND DESPERATE

Of all people, I'm probably the least likely to have an "orphan mindset." My parents were (and my mom still is) wonderfully loving, supportive, and encouraging. However, it's part of the fall that all of us, to some degree, struggle with feelings of desperation and loneliness. This is the condition God was addressing in me when He had me read about James and John coming to Jesus.

Let me be clear: When I say I struggle with an "orphan mindset," I don't want you to think I'm equating my experience with those who grew up without a mom or dad. I'm not. I'm simply saying that from a psychological perspective, even people like me, who have both parents, can have fears and insecurities that are similar to those who don't. Many of us can see the signs if we look in the mirror. Orphans lack the stability and security of a loving family, so insecurity is perhaps their most prominent characteristic. A sense of nagging fear and frantic desperation colors every moment, every decision, and every relationship. They're convinced that love is never just given; it has to be earned. They either try very hard to earn it by being good, numb the pain in some way, or attempt to fill the emptiness with various stimulations—or a combination of those behaviors.

Because they believe significance is always earned, they're naturally jealous of anyone who has achieved more or has received more acclaim. They see people as either steppingstones or hindrances to their goals. They're always checking themselves out against other people, comparing how much respect they have, so they feel either enormous superiority or self-pity—often within the same day and even within the same conversation. Anger, fear, hurt, and shame live just under the surface, and erupt like a volcano from time to time. They may be driven or helpless, or they may vacillate between the two. No matter how much success, how many possessions, how much pleasure, or how much power they accumulate, it never satisfies the deepest longings of their hearts.

As I realized how driven I'd been and how much I longed for approval, I saw an orphan mindset in me. I begged God to work in my heart to change me from the inside out, and one of the ways He answered that prayer was by bringing people to me who had the same struggle. As God gave me wisdom to speak into their lives, He was speaking into mine.

Not long after the meeting with John's board in Atlanta, I met with a young man who had come up through our youth group and had gone into the ministry. The pressure was too much for him. He couldn't handle the stress of the job and his marriage, so he began to drink to numb the pain. For a while, he was able to keep the secret, but with any addiction, a little is never enough. By the time he came to see me, his life was a train wreck.

As he poured his heart out to me, I sensed the self-pity of an orphan mindset. The Lord led me to point him to the parable of the talents. A talent was a way to measure gold or silver, about seventy pounds. Jesus told the story of a man who went on a trip and entrusted his wealth to three servants. He gave five bags of gold to one of them, two to another, and one to a third, "each according to his ability."

The one who was given five gained five more, and the one who had two earned two more, but the man who had only one "dug a hole in the ground and hid his master's money." When their master came home, he asked the servants to give an account of the money he had put in their hands. It's interesting, I explained, that the man had exactly the same response to the first two, even though one earned much more than the other. He told each one, "Well done, good and faithful servant! You have been faithful with a few things; I will put you in charge of many things. Come and share your master's happiness!" (Matthew 25:21, 23)

The lesson Jesus wants us to learn, I told the young man sitting with me, is that God is pleased when we invest our abilities with all our hearts. It's up to Him whether He gives us five or two; it's up to us what we do with the five or two. Then I looked at him and asked, "So, what does it feel like to be a two-talent guy?"

He was deeply offended. He narrowed his eyes as he insisted, "I don't know because I'm a five-talent guy."

"It's not a sin, and it's not a flaw to be a two-talent person. I sense you're discouraged because you're not accomplishing as much as people with greater gifts and skills. Let me ask you again: How does it feel to be a two-talent guy?"

He was getting upset now. He held up his hand with his fingers spread out. He again insisted he was a five-talent man.

I tried again to share the lesson God was putting on my heart: "First of all, I don't know if you're a five-talent guy or a two-talent guy, but what I do know is that if you can't be content with whatever God gives you and calls you to be, you'll never be content at all. It doesn't matter to God if He has given you five or two. His reward for faithfulness is exactly the same. It's up to Him to give us the gifts He wants to give us and put us in the place where He wants us to serve. He assigns the seats where we sit. Until we accept our place, we won't be content. We'll be driven to be on top, or we'll wallow in self-pity. We'll be frantic or depressed. We'll be fiercely competitive or we'll give up and quit. We'll try to please everybody to win approval, or we'll numb the pain. God has given you a seat. It's time you accept it."

He snarled, "That's not the seat I want!"

"I understand that." He didn't know I was so certain because this was the lesson God had been drilling into me for many years. "But if you insist that you're a five but you're really a two, you won't be either one. You've compared yourself to others, and you've taken your eyes off Jesus. You're so determined to be somebody that you're running the risk of throwing your life away and being a nobody. You're using alcohol to numb yourself and avoid the pain. It's time to go back to God, accept the seat He assigns you, and give Him your whole heart. My dad used to tell me that God's primary calling is to love Him with all my heart and love people. That's your calling, too. And I know you can do it. That's your seat. Sit there."

When he walked out the door that day, there were no signs of a desire to change the trajectory of his life, but a year later, he called and asked to see me. I wondered if I was going to hear a rebuttal a year in the making, but it wasn't that at all. He was obviously broken—in a good way. He smiled as he sat down. He told me, "I've thought about our conversation every day since we met. I'm sitting in the seat God has given me, and it's a very good place to be. I tried so hard to be a five-talent guy that I lost sight of the honor of being God's guy. I still have a long way to go. I can think I'm doing well, and then all of a sudden, I get freaked out when there's the least bit of trouble. I feel like everything could fall apart at any minute. Orphan thinking makes me want to push and shove and take and grab . . . because I feel like that's the only way to win. But God has shown me that my worry is really a sign of insecurity. I was defiant, demanding, and driven . . . until I cratered. Thank you for being honest with me."

In the Sermon on the Mount, Jesus addressed this aspect of an orphan mindset. He told the people listening,

"Therefore I tell you, do not worry about your life, what you will eat or drink; or about your body, what you will wear. Is not life more than food, and the body more than clothes? Look at the birds of the air; they do not sow or reap or store away in barns, and yet your heavenly Father feeds them. Are you not much more valuable than they? Can any one of you by worrying add a single hour to your life?" —Matthew 6:25-27

He wasn't finished. He asked them why they would worry about clothes, food, and anything else they needed, and He assured them, "For the pagans run after all these things, and your heavenly Father knows that you need them" (Matthew 6:32).

Orphans worry they won't have enough to eat, a place to sleep, or clothes to wear, and when they have those things, they worry about losing them. They expend enormous mental energy trying to figure out how to get the necessities—and how to keep people from taking them away. No matter what they have, it's never enough because the real deficit isn't food, clothes, or a bed; it's the absence of consistent, assertive love in their lives.

> **No matter what they have, it's never enough because the real deficit isn't food, clothes, or a bed; it's the absence of consistent, assertive love in their lives.**

How is an orphan mindset broken? Only by the grace of God. Jesus summed up His teaching on worry:

"But seek first his kingdom and his righteousness, and all these things will be given to you as well. Therefore do not worry about tomorrow, for tomorrow will worry about itself. Each day has enough trouble of its own." —Matthew 6:33-34

Love God, and let His affection give you the security you long for. And love people. Don't compete with them; don't compare yourself to them. Be faithful to what's in front of you, and trust God to give the only applause that really matters: "Well done! Enter the joy of your master!" You've got a loving, kind, wise, and powerful Father. You're not an orphan. Believe it. Act like it. The world may have self-made men and women, but that's not us. We're God-made, from conception to the grave. Everything we are and everything we have come from the hand of our gracious Father.

Chapter 4

Self-Sabotage

In 2001, the church board of Oaks Church voted me in as the co-pastor with my dad. We were growing, and two years later, we moved twelve miles south into a larger facility in Red Oak. The growth, the building, the pressure of the new role . . . all of this had my head spinning. To be honest, I was scared that I'd mess up something wonderful God was doing.

That year, Gerald Brooks held an annual North Texas Leadership Conference at his church in Plano. I'm sure a lot of pastors went just to get a new idea or two, but I signed up because I was desperate for answers. One of the speakers was a man named Sam Chand. He had just shifted the focus of his career from academics as the president of Beulah Heights University in Atlanta to become a consultant for pastors. I asked him to consider taking me on as a client, and to make it easy, I said, "The next time you're in town speaking for Gerald, why don't you stay over a couple of days to meet with me and speak at our church?" I didn't know until later, but before he gave me an answer, he asked Gerald about me. Gerald told him, "God is going to use Scott to do some great things. I think it's well worth your time to spend a couple of days at his church. Then you can decide if you want to sign on as a consultant."

The next October, on the Saturday after the next event at Gerald's church, Dr. Chand met with Jenni and me, and then he met with our top thirty leaders in two groups. He preached a wonderful message on Sunday, and before he flew out, Jenni and I took him to lunch. He said, "I'll give you my full assessment in a month, but I can give you a thumbnail sketch now." I was, as Ross Perot once said, all ears. He continued, "I'm very impressed with the leaders God has raised up at your church. You have potential for extraordinary growth." That's one of the things I wanted to hear. "But Scott, you have to do something really fast."

I was surprised. "Like what?"

"Your two services are packed, so you need to start a third right now."

I sat back. I had an answer for this: "Yeah, we've been thinking about doing that in January. That's when it makes the most sense."

He didn't miss a beat. "It will be too late. You will have lost momentum."

I became just a tad defensive. "It's only three months from now."

"You need to start the new service two weeks from today."

My defensiveness was morphing into fierce resistance. "No way! We can't do that! We have 120 seniors who meet with my dad in the early service. I can't just kick them out!"

"I'm not asking you to abandon them, just move them. Do you have another room where they can meet?"

"Uh, yeah. I don't know. . . ."

Dr. Chand didn't wait for me to formulate another excuse. He asked, "Would your father be open to moving the seniors to free up the worship center for another service?"

"Well, sure." He had me. "If he knew that's what we need to do to keep growing, he'd do almost anything."

Dr. Chand smiled and began giving detailed instructions: "For the room where the seniors will meet, get a very good sound system, a video projector, and comfortable chairs. Move the organ and piano there, so they feel loved and valued. You should meet with them this coming Sunday to explain the move, and they can meet in their new room the next Sunday . . . when you start your third service where they used to be."

I took a deep breath. I'm not sure what I expected of our debrief over lunch, but it sure wasn't this! I tried to sound confident, but I'm afraid my tone of voice and body language sent a different message. I said, "Dr. Chand, I'll start working on all this as soon as I drop you off at the airport. But I need more help. I really don't know what to do, but I'm willing to learn. I've told God that I'm willing to do anything He wants me to do."

I'll never forget what happened next. Dr. Chand reached across the table, put his hand on mine, and looked into my eyes. He said, "Look at me, Pastor Scott. You're going to be all right. I know what needs to be done, and I'll be with you every step of the way."

> **I took a deep breath. I'm not sure what I expected of our debrief over lunch, but it sure wasn't this!**

That was our first meeting. We continued to meet every month for the next ten years. During that time, our church grew quite a lot, but the biggest growth was in me.

And yes, we started the third service two weeks after having lunch with Dr. Chand. We grew by five hundred people that year. I'm convinced this level of growth wouldn't have happened if we hadn't started the third service when we did.

When Dr. Chand came back to give me his full assessment, he came with both barrels loaded. He handed me a bound stack of papers and said, "From my time with you, Jenni, and your leaders, I've identified thirty-eight specific steps you can take. All of them will lead to more growth." He went through them one by one, in great detail. When he finished, I put my head in my hands. I wanted to cry. How could he see so many holes in our church's life in only two days with us? I was sure that he had concluded I was the most horrible pastor in the history of the Christian faith. He saw that I was distraught. Again, he reached over and put his hand on mine. He said, "Pastor Scott, don't worry. I've got you. I'll show you how to do all this."

Dr. Chand gave me a couple of months to chew on his lengthy assessment. He knew my capacity wasn't big enough to handle all thirty-eight recommendations from the get-go, so he focused on three: a poverty mindset, a Jesus complex, and the fear of disapproval.

A POVERTY MINDSET

When we met in January, Dr. Chand asked, "How much are you going to raise this year above the general fund?"

I was ready. "We need $250,000 to build an entrance to our property to satisfy the city code, and this construction has to connect seamlessly with the new bridge being built over the interstate in front of us. We have to get this done."

He always carries a legal pad. He wrote "$250,000" on it, and then he asked, "What else?"

I was confused. I said, "That's it. That's what we need, and it'll be enough of a stretch."

He asked, "So, you don't have any needs beyond that?"

"Well," my mind started racing. "Well, uh, yeah, we could use a lot more if we could raise it."

"Okay," he had his pen ready. "Like what?"

"I'd love to finish out the kids' area."

"How much would that cost?"

"I think we could do it for $100,000."

He wrote it under the other number. It was looking suspiciously like a list in the making. He looked up. "What else?"

"Well, it would be great if we could have an outreach next year at Halloween to reach families in our community."

"How much would that cost?"

"Oh, I don't. . . ."

"What's your best estimate?"

"Maybe $50,000 to rent a carnival."

He wrote it down, and then he asked again, "What else?"

This was sounding like pie-in-the-sky dreaming, but I was willing (barely) to go along. I told him, "We could use some money for missions. We have about $300,000 worth of projects on hold with our missionary partners because we haven't had the money for them."

Dr. Chand wrote it down, and then he looked at me and said, "Pastor Scott, you could raise all that money and more—much more."

It was time for my skepticism to slow the bus down. I shook my head and assured him, "Dr. Chand, we have a lot of new believers in our church, and I don't want them to think all I care about is their money. And besides, we just came out of a three-year capital campaign. Our people have 'giving fatigue.'"

He nodded. I thought my points were irrefutable, and the discussion was over. It wasn't. He insisted, "I understand, but $250,000 is too low. Your people have much more capacity for giving than that."

I pulled out my big gun: "No offense, Dr. Chand." (You know, whenever anybody says, "No offense," you can be sure they're going to be offensive.) "You're a lot smarter than me, and you're an expert in leadership and church growth, but I'm pretty sure I know my people better than you do."

I don't know if he took offense, but it didn't look like it. He put his pen down and smiled as he explained, "Pastor Scott, trust me. I know what I'm talking about. This is why you asked me to be your consultant. Your growth is blocked by a poverty mindset. If you let me show you how to cast the vision and lead people to hear from God, you could raise $800,000 in the next eight weeks."

This moment, I instantly realized, was a pivotal point in our relationship. I could trust him and take steps forward, or I could walk away from his input into my life. We might continue to meet, but it would never be the same. I took a deep breath and announced, "It's really hard for me to get my head around it, but I'll listen to you, and I'll do what you say."

When Dr. Chand said "the next eight weeks," that's exactly what he meant. Immediately, he helped me map out a plan to cast vision

> **This moment, I instantly realized, was a pivotal point in our relationship.**

for meeting all of these needs, teach people about giving, and encourage them to seek God's direction and step out in faith. He could tell my heart was still hesitant, so he asked, "Pastor Scott, do you love your people and want them to grow in their faith?"

"Yes, certainly. With all my heart."

"What's holding you back from helping them grow in their giving?"

I was ready. "That's easy. I don't want ours to be one of those churches that badgers people about money. I don't want to scare new Christians away. And I don't want to offend people who have just given so much for our new building."

He nodded, but I could tell it wasn't that he agreed with my conclusion. He asked, "Pastor Scott, do you ever preach on topics of spiritual growth and obedience that could offend someone?"

"Well, yes, but that's different?"

"Tell me about that."

"The Bible has a lot of guardrails to keep people from ruining their lives: adultery, lying, selfishness, jealousy, greed, heaven and hell, Jesus is the only hope of salvation—I talk about these things all the time, along with the grace of God to forgive and restore."

He leaned in: "Doesn't the Bible have a lot of guardrails about money?" Before I could respond, he answered his own question. "There are more than 2,300 verses about money, wealth, and possessions. About 15 percent of Jesus' preaching is about money, and eleven of the thirty-nine parables are about it. It's the topic He spoke about most often." He looked at me and asked, "Pastor Scott, why do you think Jesus talked so much about money?"

He had me again. "Because it's so easy to get messed up about money."

"What do you mean by 'messed up'?"

I rattled off many of the things I'd mentioned earlier and added a few more: "Selfishness, jealousy, greed, debt, dishonesty, and the idolatry of making money and possessions more important than God."

"Pastor Scott, do people need God's instruction about these things?" I nodded. "Do they need to grow in those areas?" I kept nodding. "Then look at it this way: You aren't trying to get people to give. You're trying to help people grow in their faith and obedience."

That made perfect sense to me, and it radically shifted my thinking.

He asked, "How will you teach your people to grow in their faith and obedience regarding giving?"

"The same way I teach about anything. I'll use the Scriptures and teach with authority, I'll use illustrations, and I'll use examples of people who give gladly and generously."

He pointed at me and said, "And you'll model it. You and Jenni have to lead the way. You are the 'lead followers' at your church. Paul said, 'Follow me as I follow Christ,' and he said, 'Think the way I think, and do what I do, and you'll be following Jesus.'"

"Okay, I get it. Jenni and I need to give a lot of money to kick this off."

Dr. Chand tilted his head and explained, "Yes, but it's more than that. You need to model what it looks like to pray, to seek God for direction, and to obey His voice. And as you know well, it's important to model the commitment to step out in faith even if, like Abraham, you don't see how it can ever work out." He paused for a second, and then gave the punchline: "You need to model what it looks like to need a miracle."

"I'm not sure. . . ."

He jumped back in: "We live in safe and predictable ways. We have so many comforts that we expect spiritual life to always be easy and comfortable. That's not what we see in the Scriptures or in church history. Great leaders—and great Christians—are willing to trust God to do something they couldn't possibly do on their own."

He took out his pen again, and he said, "Okay, let's come up with a plan. The whole thing starts with prayer." He started writing.

"And listening in prayer. And being committed to obey . . . to do whatever God tells us to do."

He gave the bottom line: "Pastor Scott, it's your job to set God up for a miracle, to put yourself in a place where the only way to do what God has told you to do is for Him to make it happen in a supernatural way. And everyone will see it, from beginning to end. And the people will say, 'Wow!'"

That was the last thing he wrote down. He had "pray," "listen," "obey," and "wow."

I thought for a few seconds and then said, "That spells PLOW."

"Look at that. It sure does."

I continued, "That fits perfectly. God wants to plow up the soil of our hearts, so we can be prepared to receive His Word and reap a miracle. Okay, I get it. That's what God wants to do in all this: plow our hearts to get us ready to do a miracle. We pray, listen, and obey—that's our part. And God brings the Wow, the miracle. He's the Wow Factor."

"Is that your plan, Pastor Scott?"

"Yeah, that's our plan. I love that!"

After he left, I started putting all the pieces together. I met with our staff team and our board to share the vision, and we planned to kick it off a month later. In my first message to the church, I shared the PLOW process with them, and I told them how Jenni and I had prayed, listened, and obeyed God's clear call for us to give $10,000 over our regular giving. I explained that we didn't have that much lying around in a bank account or under the mattress, but we believed God would provide. We were going to cut out a lot of extra expenses like eating out, but that wouldn't come close to the $10,000. I asked our people to PLOW during the next week and make a commitment to trust God for whatever He put on their hearts. I explained their part and God's part, and I told them, "Everybody wants to see God do a miracle, but nobody wants to be in a position to need one. I'm asking you to position yourself for a miracle."

Over the next eight weeks, we saw miracle after miracle. People shared that they got promotions and unexpected raises. Some were surprised to receive inheritances from family members they didn't even know. A few got money back because they'd overpaid a bill or got a tax refund. Teenagers mowed lawns and did other kinds of chores for their neighbors, and people gave them big tips when the kids shared their goal to raise money for missions. Some of our parents and grand-parents were touched by our effort to finish the kids' area, and others were excited about the outreach planned for Halloween. Every week, I shared a story about God doing a miracle to provide. And after each story, our people learned to say in unison, "Wow!"

It took a little longer than eight weeks to raise the $800,000, but that was perfectly fine with me. We got to do all the things Dr. Chand and I had put on the list, but I realized that the amount people gave wasn't as important as the faith generated in the hearts of our people. The next time Dr. Chand came, I told him, "You were right. It's more about helping people grow in faith and obedience than about the money."

He said, "Pastor Scott, I'm so proud of you. You stepped out in faith and led the campaign. You helped your people grow in their faith and their generosity. Well done!" Then he told me with a grin on his face,

"When I left our first meeting, I was fully aware of what my biggest problem was going to be in seeing Oaks Church grow to its full potential. Do you know what it was?" I shook my head. He said, "I knew it was going to be YOU."

I wasn't at all offended. I knew he was right, and he wasn't being malicious in the least. He continued, "Your people want to give, they want to serve, they want to make a difference, and they want to grow in their faith, but you were so scared for them. You wanted to protect them, but in some ways you were protecting them from God. Think about it: They wanted to give, and the money was there. God was waiting to unleash miracles, but none of it could happen until your insecurity got out of the way. To your credit, you grew. You gave them the opportunity to trust God, and they took it." He stopped for a few seconds, and then gave me his conclusion: "Your church can't outgrow you. When you grow, they can grow. There's no other way around it. You are the lid on the potential growth of your church."

> **My insecurity was sabotaging growth . . . in me, in my team, and in my church.**

My insecurity was sabotaging growth . . . in me, in my team, and in my church. The principle doesn't apply only to pastors and their churches. It applies to parents and their children, as well as to leaders at any level of any organization. It was a vital lesson, but it wasn't the only one Dr. Chand would teach me.

A SAVIOR COMPLEX

Several months after I began meeting with Dr. Chand, I started experiencing panic attacks: racing thoughts, labored breathing, sweating, rapid heartbeat, and an acute fear something terrible was about to happen. I told him about it.

He said, "I have a degree in counseling, but that's not my role in your life. You need a counselor. There are areas of your life where you need to grow, and the only way to make progress is with a professional counselor."

Okay, that confirmed what I thought. I asked, "Where do I find one?"

He said, "The same way you do anything else: you ask, you seek, you knock, and the door will be opened to you."

"But what if. . . ."

"What if you don't connect with the first person you try? Go to someone else, and someone else until you find the right fit."

I called some friends to ask for a recommendation. I wanted to find someone who was a gifted counselor, not just a nice person, a believer if possible, with an office at least thirty minutes away, who didn't come to our church and wasn't part of our denomination. One of my friends highly recommended a counselor who seemed to fit the criteria. I called and set up an appointment.

A few days later, I walked into the counselor's office and sat down.

He asked, "Scott, how can I help you?"

I told him, "I'm a pastor . . . actually a co-pastor at a church with my dad. I have a big problem."

I'm sure his mind was spinning with all the options of what people talk about in his office, but he only asked, "What is it?"

"I hate Sundays."

He didn't react. He only said, "That must be really hard on you."

At that moment, the torrents of tears were unleashed. I couldn't even talk.

He said, "Take your time. We're in no hurry."

After a few minutes, I had enough composure to explain: "Almost every week, someone calls the church to ask if I'm preaching the next Sunday. When I say, 'yes,' they say, 'Please make sure it's really good. I'm bringing a friend who doesn't know Jesus, and I want to be sure this will be a good week to bring him.' This happens almost every week, and it freaks me out! If I don't preach well, I let our church member down, and worse, the person who's visiting may not trust in Jesus . . . because of me."

I started crying again. He handed me a tissue and said, "That's a lot of pressure. It must be hard to be responsible for so many souls. Their eternity is in your hands, and it all depends on your delivering a good message . . . or not." He paused for a few seconds and then asked, "So, where does Jesus fit in this picture?"

"What do you mean?" I asked. "Jesus is involved in everything we do."

He raised his eyebrows and mused, "Well, that's not what I'm hearing. It sounds like it's all on you. He'll save them, but first it's up to you to convince them. Your message has to be good enough for them to believe. In fact, it has to be pretty close to perfect. Isn't that what you told me?"

I wasn't sure how to answer. He continued, "Doesn't the Bible say that no one comes to Christ unless the Spirit draws them?" I nodded. It seemed more than a bit odd that the counselor I'd known for less than fifteen minutes was teaching the Bible to me. He kept going, "Well, then, the Spirit draws and Jesus saves. What part do you play?"

"I share the gospel."

He shifted gears a little. "Let me ask you a question, Scott. I bet that you get in the car every Sunday after the service and ask Jenni to rank your message on a scale of one to ten. Isn't that how it happens?"

"No." I tried to sound confident, but I was smiling. "Sometimes we don't ride together. But yeah, that's pretty much how our conversation goes at some point . . . in the car, at lunch, or at home."

"So, what scores does she give you?"

"Sometimes pretty high, sometimes not."

"Do you know what happens?" he asked, but I knew he would answer his own question. "When you score a ten, it becomes the new five. If you hit it once, you should be able to hit it every time. That adds to the pressure because you always have to do better to score higher than a five. You've got a scoring system that shifts upward when you do well. It's a flawed system, but it's what you've been living with. It's exhausting. It's crushing. Do you know what I'm talking about, Scott?"

"Exactly. That's why I'm here."

He said, "But actually, that's not the question you should be asking."

"Oh, yeah? What's the right question?"

"It depends," he explained. "Do you want to keep score the way heaven keeps score?" I nodded. I wasn't sure where this was going, but I wanted to find out. He continued, "What's the number one value of heaven?"

I answered, "Love. Paul said it doesn't matter how great your gifts are, how much you give away, or even if you die a martyr's death, without love, it's all meaningless and empty."

"Okay, then, if you want to keep score like heaven does, you should ask Jenni, 'How well did I love them this week?'"

It was a revelation. Instantly, I knew it would radically change how I saw myself and my responsibilities.

He then said, "And do you know what, Scott? I've known you for less than an hour, but I can tell you'll get a ten every week." Instantly, his words touched me deeply. He added, "People don't remember what you say, but they certainly remember how they felt when you said it—and I'm quite sure they feel loved when you speak to them."

The tears flowed again. I told him, "That's all I want. I want to please God and let people know how much He loves them."

He said, "Start keeping score the way heaven does. Scott, just tell people that Jesus died to save them. The Scriptures will convince them, the Holy Spirit will draw them, and your job is to love them."

Finally, I was able to see that I had shouldered the responsibility that only Jesus can carry—to save the lost by delivering perfect and powerful messages—and the weight was killing me. I had developed a Jesus complex, but in only one meeting with the counselor, he held up a mirror for me to see my faulty thinking.

When Dr. Chand came for his next visit, I told him about my meeting with the counselor. I said, "And that was just our first meeting. I'm planning to keep seeing him for a long time . . . maybe the rest of my life."

Dr. Chand told me, "Pastor Scott, you're gifted. To be a pastor, you have to have talent, but I've seen a lot of talented leaders who never reached their full potential because they weren't willing to deal with the deep issues of their souls. They worked on the business of the church, but they didn't give attention to their hearts. Here's something to remember: your talent can bring you success, but your character keeps you from losing it."

My panic attacks were a loud and clear signal that I was again my own worst enemy. Crushing expectations had been sabotaging my effectiveness and my joy. Finally, a load was lifted from my shoulders.

FEAR OF DISAPPROVAL

After Dr. Chand and I had been meeting over a year, he told me about the importance of having an "Honesty Policy." I didn't think I needed it because I'm not known as a liar. He said it goes deeper than that: "Pastor Scott, when I met with your leaders on that first Saturday when I came to your church, I sensed that some of your people feel hesitant to be completely honest with you. You don't like conflict. You love people, and you want them to get along with each other. Unity, however, isn't uniformity. You have to teach them how to be honest with each other without attacking or being defensive."

"Okay, but how do I do that?"

He said, "Install an honesty policy with your team that says, 'I will speak the truth in love to the last ten percent, to the right person, at the right time, in the right way, and we will not tolerate gossip among our leadership.' Have them read it, talk about it, and sign it. Then, at the end of every meeting, tell them, 'Thank you for your leadership and your commitment to serve God and our church. Jesus said the gates of hell will not prevail against us as long as we're unified. So, we need to guard against confusion, distrust, and division . . . in any form. If there's anything in your heart that's unsettled, if you think an idea is off target, or we're going in a wrong direction, or if someone has offended you, I'm asking you to put it all on the table. All of it. If we're transparent, we can discuss anything, resolve issues, and walk in unity.'"

Dr. Chand suggested I read it to the team and the board at the first of every year and have them recommit to it. It's easy to drift, so all of us need this reminder.

And that's exactly what we did. I think everyone on the team was at least a little like me—pretty excited about the possibility of being really honest with each other, but more than a little apprehensive about what it would look like. I asked the people on our staff team and those on our board to sign the statement.

At the end of our staff and board meetings, I always ask, "Have you been honest to the last ten percent? Is there anything we need to talk about?" This simple statement—and the willingness to affirm those who speak up—has had a very positive effect on all of us. From the first time, we were off and running—with one exception.

Charles had been on our board for a long time. He believed he had the gift of rebuke. He saw his role as a devil's advocate to question everything . . . and I mean everything. No matter how positive and productive our conversation had been about an idea, he always jumped in, "Pastor Scott, I'm sorry to say it, but I don't see it like that." It happened in every board meeting. One time, he voted "no" on a relatively minor decision. We always tried to talk things through to have a consensus, and in this case, the rest of us felt we were in tune with the heart and mind of God. Charles was the only "no." I asked him what his objections were. He hadn't voiced any concerns about the concept during our discussion, and I was confused that he had a problem with it now. He explained, "I just don't like it that we always have unanimous votes. It makes our board look weak. I wanted to vote "no" to show that we can disagree with each other."

I ended the meeting with a statement of the honesty policy. After we adjourned, I asked Charles if we could talk. When everyone else had left, I told him, "I'm not sure why you feel compelled to consistently disagree with whatever decision we're making."

He hardly waited for me to finish: "We need healthy discussion. The guys in there go along with whatever you think we should do. I'm the only one who's willing to play devil's advocate and push back."

I asked, "Why would you want to be his advocate?"

"You know what I mean."

"Yes, I know what you mean, but I'd prefer you to be an advocate for truth. I welcome disagreement, but constructive disagreement, not just for the sake of being a contrarian. I'd like all of us, including you, to pray and seek God's wisdom, to voice our hopes and our concerns, and to try to come up with the very best plan to advance God's kingdom."

"That's what I'm doing."

I obviously didn't buy it. I didn't correct him, but I continued, "It would help if you could give me and the others the benefit of the doubt. You could say, 'You've probably already thought of this, but here's a concern I have.' Or you could say, 'Help me understand this a little more clearly.' Or 'I really like where this is going. How will we handle this issue or that one?' Do you see the difference? I'm very happy for you to speak to the heart of what we're doing, and I want you to be 100 percent with us on the journey to the best decisions. We don't need 'no' votes just to make a statement that we can disagree. That's why we have the honesty policy. I expect people to disagree, but I expect them to be constructive in the discussion. Let me be honest to the last ten percent with you, Charles. When I see you getting ready to speak up in the meeting, joy doesn't flood my soul. I think, *Oh, great. Here we go again.* That's not what I want to think and feel. I'd love for us to walk away from this meeting with a new commitment to be both honest and constructive. I'm willing. Are you?"

I thought I'd made the point pretty well. I hoped he'd say, "I see what you mean. I'm going to pray about it, and I'm making a commitment right now to be a positive force on the board." But that's not how he responded. He told me, "Pastor, God has been telling me that I don't fit on the board. He doesn't want me to serve there any longer."

I assured him, "That's not what I'm asking you to do. You're smart and gifted, and you bring a lot to our board. But if that's what God is saying to you, why don't you tell the board next month that you're stepping off, but you're available to come back when and if the Lord leads you in the future?"

A month later, Charles came. I invited him to share his thoughts with the rest of the board, and he said, "God told me to step off the board and that I'll never serve here in this way again." He had to be contrary even in his last words to the board. I affirmed him and thanked him for serving with us, we prayed for him, and he left the meeting.

This was an important moment for me and my role as a leader. The rest of the people on the board sensed that there had been an honest conversation between Charles and me sometime before this meeting. They realized the honesty policy wasn't just talk. I was willing to live by it, and our conversations rose to a new level of transparency.

Before Dr. Chand told me about the honesty policy, I would never have had the conversation with Charles. I would have stewed about his negativity. I would have complained to Jenni, and Charles would have burned up a truckload of my mental energy. "To the last ten percent" is the key concept. It means we voice "those little things that bug us" instead of letting them eat away at our hearts like a corrosive acid.

We still do this. It's always the last item on the agenda. I always read our honesty policy and invite people to voice any concerns they haven't shared during the meeting. It's gold.

No, I don't lie very much, but Dr. Chand helped me see that I had an aversion to telling the truth when it wasn't going to be received gladly. I needed the honesty policy as much as any of the rest of the people on our team and the board. He taught me that when I avoid the discomfort of wading into sticky problems, it's not wisdom. It's cowardice, and each time, I leak credibility. Leadership functions only at the level of credibility.

SPOTS

Dr. Chand is amazingly perceptive. He has taught me that all leaders have blind spots, deaf spots, and dumb spots. These are ways we self-sabotage. We don't see the truth that's right in front of us because we don't want to see it. We prefer to live in a world of false assumptions because they don't demand hard decisions. We aren't willing to hear feedback from people who know more than we do. Confirmation bias isn't just in politics. It's easy for all of us to hear only what reinforces what we already believe, and we discount any competing (or correcting) messages. And, we don't speak the truth that needs to be voiced, the hard truth, the inconvenient truth, the awkward truth. We prefer to think we're kind, but we're really just scared. Making people happy is more important to our sense of identity as "a nice person and a good leader" than wading into the messiness of people's lives to help them learn to live in truth and grace.

Before Dr. Chand began meeting with me, I had no idea I was limiting our church and hindering our people's faith with my poverty mindset. He was absolutely right: I was protecting them—I thought I was protecting them from being needlessly hurt, but I was preventing them from trusting God for greater things. I was sure my misplaced burden in preaching was exactly what God wanted for me. It showed, I believed, my zeal and passion—but it was eating me alive. And I never had the slightest concept of pushing myself and others to be honest to the last ten percent. If Dr. Chand hadn't shared this idea with me, I

> **He has taught me that all leaders have blind spots, deaf spots, and dumb spots. These are ways we self-sabotage.**

would have continued to shade my conversations to limit conflict, so people would see me as a really nice person. That had been my real goal.

I believe all leaders, no matter the size of the organization or the age of the leader, need a consultant and a counselor. Consultants can help us take our people, our churches, and our companies farther than we can take them on our own, and counselors can take us to places of healing and strength that we didn't even know existed.

Chapter 5

God Picked Me

When Dad and I had been co-pastors for about five years, we realized it was time for a shift in responsibilities. Dad had launched a charter school about eight years earlier, and it was doing incredibly well. At this point, both of us were splitting our time between the church and the school. Both of them were growing, and we were stretched thin. One day I told him, "Dad, it's time for you to concentrate on the school and for me to focus on the church. I'll be glad to help you anyway I can, but for a number of reasons, I think this move is the wise thing for us to do."

One of the reasons was our reputation. At the time, some charter schools were being criticized for poor financial management. Our salaries were entirely aboveboard, but I didn't want anyone to blow a gasket because we were receiving incomes from both organizations. My plan was for me to receive all of my income from the church and Dad to receive his income entirely from the school.

Pastoral succession is often an awkward and difficult time in the life of a church. In some ways, this one looked like it would be easy because

I was already the co-pastor, and Dad had a vital role in the school. But looks are deceiving. I had been anticipating this moment for a long time. I knew where to expect some real tension, and I suspected this process would lead us through a minefield of expectations and emotions. I wanted to take slow, careful steps.

But I knew someone with a superpower: Sam Chand. I asked him to help us find a path through the minefield, so we wouldn't set off any explosions . . . or at least we'd minimize them. He and I met to consider the plan. He explained, "Pastor Scott, succession is very difficult in most organizations for three reasons: money, identity, and marriage. In the church, many pastors haven't saved enough money over the years to comfortably retire. They hang on to their roles long past the time they should have moved on, but they don't want to tell their people this is the reason they want to stay. They come up with other reasons—a myriad of reasons—to slow down or stop church leaders from looking for a successor. The second reason is identity. Most pastors have given their lives, or at least many years, to the people in their churches. Their sense of who they are is tied up in the respect of their people, the building, and the things God has done through them. Apart from their role at the church, who are they? They don't have an answer to that question. They've never developed any other sense of themselves, so it's terribly threatening for them to think about leaving. In fact, it feels like a kind of death. The third major reason succession is difficult is that many pastors and their spouses have spent decades in separate spheres. Spending a lot of time together may sound wonderful to some people, but it's a major adjustment for many pastors and their spouses. In fact, I'm not sure who dreads it most!" He paused for a few seconds and then asked,

"Do we need to address any of these factors in the pastoral succession at your church?"

I thought for a while, and then I responded, "I think my mom and dad are okay together, and he's going to receive a salary from the school, so that's not an issue. The problem is going to be his identity.He has been a respected pastor for forty years. That's his life, that's his calling, that's who he is. Yeah, that's going to be a tough one."

Dr. Chand assured me, "We'll work through that, so he feels honored. Maybe he can have the title of pastor emeritus or something likethat. We want him to know you and the church value him."

"That's exactly what I want. I want to honor my dad in every possible way."

Dr. Chand said, "I'll lead the conversation. Don't worry. We'll find a way through this."

The next day, the three of us sat down. Dad wasn't blindsided. He knew what was coming, and he obviously had been anticipating this meeting. Dr. Chand began, "Dr. Tom, you have done an incredible job raising Scott to be a great leader. You have prepared him to assume the leadership of the church, and now, you will take the school to a higher level. You'll have even more impact on children and their parents. Scott is ready for this transition, and so are you."

Dad sat with a grim look on his face. He was nodding, but not in glad agreement. When Dr. Chand finished, Dad sat back in his chair and growled, "Well, I knew this day would come."

Dr. Chand said only, "Really?"

Someone pushed a button on Dad, and a prerecorded message came out. He turned to me and said, "I've never told you, Scott, but years ago when you were rising in your leadership, I had appointments with two counselors. I told the first one, 'My son is very gifted, and one day he's going to be a phenomenal pastor. But I'm wondering, should I keep him on my team? If he stays, I'm pretty sure he'll outgrow me.' The counselor told me, 'I know Scott, and you're absolutely right. You need to get him out of there right now! If you don't, he's going to eat you alive, take over, and kick you to the sidelines.' I thought, *That's a hard statement. It may be true, but I'm not sure.*"

It took every ounce of self-control I could muster to keep from saying, "What are you talking about? I had no idea you felt threatened by me!" But I kept my mouth shut. Dad didn't.

He continued, "So, I went to another counselor and told him the whole story. He said, 'Scott will absolutely surpass you, and one day, he'll take over.' I asked, 'So, do you think I should get rid of him?' He answered, 'Pastor Tom, this is everything you've hoped and dreamed for your son and your church. He'll come after you and take the church to another level. He'll be a huge blessing to you, and you'll be so proud of him. Get rid of him? No, celebrate him instead.'"

Dad looked at Dr. Chand and then me, and then he said, "I want you both to know that I went with the second guy. I'm ready right now, and Son, I'm going to give you the church."

Maybe I should have felt relieved that Dad was agreeing to the transition, but I was immensely frustrated. How could he have gone to counselors to determine if he wanted to keep me on his staff team? I had given my life to serve him and help him fulfill his dreams! Did he really think I was trying to steal the role of pastor from him? It was like a huge curtain had been pulled back on my entire time serving with my dad, and I didn't like what I saw.

MENTAL BLOCK

Dr. Chand helped us with the transition, and I was made the lead pastor at Oaks Church. But one sentence from the meeting with Dr. Chand and my dad stayed stuck on replay in my mind. It was when Dad told me, "I'm going to give you the church." I wish I could say that I prayed about it, and the fear went away, but that's not what happened. Oh, I prayed, but they were anxious prayers. I had nightmares and dark daydreams of my dad walking into my office and telling me he was taking the church back. He was following the first counselor's advice after all! Based on his statement, this anxiety made perfect sense: If Dad gave the church to me, he could take it away.

But there's a corollary fear: If Dad gave it to me, I'm on my own to figure things out and make the church grow. Whenever anything didn't go perfectly at the church (Hello! We work with fallen people in a fallen world.), I interpreted the moment as the final straw, the determining factor showing that I shouldn't have been made the pastor. Every set back, every delay, and every disagreement became a cataclysmic threat to my identity and my role. I expected to see Dad walk into my office at any time to kick me to the curb and take over again. Every time the phone rang and I saw his name on caller ID, I wondered, *Is this it?*

Those weren't fleeting thoughts. They were a poisonous cloud in my mind that sometimes lifted, but not for long. During all that time, I didn't connect the two

> Every setback, every delay, and every disagreement became a cataclysmic threat to my identity and my role.

obvious dots: my vivid imaginations that Dad would come back to take over . . . and his statement in the meeting with Dr. Chand that he was "giving" the church to me.

After years of living with those fears, I attended a pastors' retreat. During a break as people milled around, a man I'd never met sat in a chair in front of me. He turned and said, "God wants you to know that He's the one who called you and placed you in your role as a pastor."

I said, "That's great. Thanks." I had no idea why he said that to me.

He then told me, "The Lord wants you to know, it wasn't the church that called you, it's not the board, and it's not your dad. Your dad didn't give you the church. God did."

Instantly, I burst into tears. He let me cry a while, and then he said, "You need to hear it again. God is the one who has made you the pastor at your church. Your dad couldn't give it to you because it wasn't his to give. The Father gave it to you."

He let it sink in, and then he said, "We're going to pray it through. I want you to say this with me: My heavenly Father called me and appointed me as the pastor of Oaks Church. If He appointed me, He will empower me."

I said it with him.

Then he said, "Let's say it again."

And we did.

"One more time."

And we said it together a third time.

He stood up, put his hands on me and prayed, "God, we break all the lies of the enemy. In Jesus' name, we come against the deception put on this young man: the doubts, the fears, the anxiety, the insecurity. Give him joy and strength."

I understand that fears can actually be lodged in a part of the brain, and when that happens, it's very difficult to completely remove them. That makes sense to me. After the retreat, the nightmares became much less frequent; although, I still had them from time to time. When they happened, though, I wasn't traumatized. I now had the weapons of truth, assurance, and confidence that God had me right where He wanted me to be. I was still in a fight, but I wasn't defenseless any longer.

STEWARDSHIP, NOT OWNERSHIP

I've had to do a lot of thinking about God's calling. It's easy to get things mixed up, with disastrous results. God calls us first to *Himself*—as His loved, forgiven, treasured child. If nothing else in our lives goes the way we want it to, we have this bedrock of certainty. In John's first letter, I can almost hear him shout: "See what great love the Father has lavished on us, that we should be called children of God! And that is what we are!" (1 John 3:1) He then explained that our grasp of this relationship gives us hope for the future and holiness in the present:

Dear friends, now we are children of God, and what we will be has not yet been made known. But we know that when Christ appears, we shall be like him, for we shall see him as he is. All who have this hope in him purify themselves, just as he is pure. —vv. 2-3

Second, we're called to a *cause*. God has made us junior partners in the family business: seeking and saving the lost, making disciples of all nations, and establishing a new kingdom of kindness, justice, and righteousness on earth. But we have to get the order right: we are called first to God and then to His cause. In his book *The Call*, Os Guinness defined our calling as "the truth that God calls us to himself so decisively that everything we are, everything we do, and everything we have is invested with a special devotion and dynamism lived out as a response to his summons and service."[2] That's the right order.

Finally, God calls us to a *place* where we invest the talents He has entrusted to us. If we believe our primary calling is to a place, the success of our efforts (or lack of it) becomes the source of our identity. When things are going well, we feel good, we feel strong, we feel valuable. When things aren't going well, we become anxious. We react by running around to fix things to make people happy with us. We muscle up to intimidate people and we insist on respect. Or we're filled with shame and self-pity, ready to give up. And some of us are so threatened, we do all of these!

If we try to get our identity from some place, we'll do whatever it takes to get on top and stay on top. We'll always be checking ourselves out and comparing our success to our peers', afraid we'll come up short. We'll name-drop, position ourselves to look good, and hang out with people who tell us what we want to hear.

When our calling is out of order, everything is about us, not God, and not even the people we lead. Our goal is to prove ourselves—to ourselves, to our peers, to our parents, or to our people—and we use every conceivable method to accomplish that goal. Of course, we see even mild criticism and constructive feedback as a personal attack because it shakes the foundation of our self-esteem: our stellar performance. That's how we want people to see us, and that's how we want to see ourselves. But there's a catch. Performance is a cruel master. The applause it brings satisfies for a moment, but it inevitably leaves us feeling empty and longing for more.

I know what I'm talking about because that's a perfect description of me.

---

2 Os Guinness, *The Call*, (Nashville: Word Publishing, 1998), 4.

I had to realize that my dad didn't own Oaks Church, and when he "gave" it to me, I didn't own it either. I'm a steward of what God has given me. God is the shepherd; I'm the under-shepherd. My calling as His child surpasses everything else. It's more wonderful, more glorious, more hopeful, more inspiring, more comforting, and more challenging than any task He might give me to do. If belonging to the King of creation thrills my soul, then I'll devote my all to the cause, and to be honest, I won't really care what the place may be. I'm thrilled to serve Him anywhere, anytime, in any role.

Even before my encounter with the pastor at the retreat, I tried to burn these concepts into my heart. Every morning when I got to my office, I walked around and prayed, "God, this isn't my office. It's Your office. I just get to use it today. The moment You tell me it's time for someone else to be here, that's fine with me. I'll follow You anywhere." Before I stepped on the platform every Sunday morning, I prayed, "Lord, You want me to love these people well. They're Your people, not my people. I'm going to tell them what You've given me to tell them today, and I'm going to love them, but if anything great is going to happen in their lives, it's because of You, not me." Before staff meetings, I prayed, "God, these are Your staff members. It's not up to me to keep them when You open a door for them to serve in another role. My job is to point them to You and let You lead them. The people on my staff aren't serving me to promote my reputation and make me successful. They're Yours. They're serving You, promoting Your reputation, and expanding Your kingdom."

One of the reasons I pray this way so often is to combat the nightmares and the anxiety. I believe we learn the most and grow the most in times of suffering. Those painful years forced me to cling to the right sequence of calling. Still, it took the breakthrough at the retreat to finally begin to free myself from the enemy's bondage to lies and fear.

ALL OF US

The problem of getting the order of calling out of whack certainly isn't limited to pastors and churches. One of the biggest errors in the church world is the assumption that full-time Christian workers are "called by God," and everybody else is just filling seats and giving money for pastors, staff, and missionaries to do God's work. Thankfully, that misconception has been shattered in most churches, but I'm not sure we've done a good enough job communicating the order of calling to everybody in the church.

Christians in business can have their calling out of order. The demands and benefits of work are visible every day, and can begin to consume their lives. If they see their work as their primary calling, they neglect their relationship with God, and they even neglect their families.

Parents love their kids, but when their children become the center of their lives, parents smother them, demand too much of them, and make their decisions for them "to protect them." But that's not protecting them; it's protecting the parents' reputations.

Jenni and I have wrestled with this. We love our kids dearly, but we realize they're the Lord's, and we only have them for a few years. It's our privilege for God to entrust them to us for a while so we can disciple them. Our goal, like God's goal for us, is for them to love God supremely and have Him be the bedrock of their security. Then, we hope they're gripped with God's cause to redeem and restore lost humanity. When they get those right, we're confident God will lead them to a place where He wants them to serve. Sounds simple, doesn't it? It's a privilege, but it's also a huge challenge for parents to gradually shift responsibility to the growing, maturing children—knowing when and how to let them fail, so they'll become wiser, stronger, and more confident next time.

We have choices every day to get our calling right. The world (and many Christians) value secondary things more than primary things. Through Jeremiah, God reminds us of the right order. In the Scriptures, a "boast" reveals what a person depends on and delights in. God told His people six centuries before Christ, and He tells us today:

"Let not the wise boast of their wisdom or the strong boast of their strength or the rich boast of their riches, but let the one who boasts boast about this: that they have the understanding to know me, that I am the LORD, who exercises kindness, justice and righteousness on earth, for in these I delight," declares the LORD." —Jeremiah 9:23-24

All around us, people boast of their intellect, their power and prestige, and their wealth and possessions. God says to you and me, "You're different. You have something bigger and better to live for. You have Me!" And when we know Him, we'll want to be like Him. Instead of ignoring or dominating people, we'll be kind. Instead of being selfish, we'll care for the disadvantaged. Instead of cutting corners on ethics, we'll

Instead of ignoring or dominating people, we'll be kind. Instead of being selfish, we'll care for the disadvantaged. Instead of cutting corners on ethics, we'll speak the truth no matter what it costs. That's a person who is living out God's calling.

speak the truth no matter what it costs. That's a person who is living out God's calling.

These are hard lessons for me, but it appears they are hard lessons for all of us. It's human nature to use external things to give us the security only God can give. It's a fight every day to keep our heads screwed on right and our hearts fixed on Jesus.

My insecurities surfaced during and after a pastoral transition at our church. It's safe to say that if Dr. Chand hadn't been in the middle of it all, it would have been a disaster. His wisdom and objectivity allowed him to see what my dad and I couldn't see, to say what we weren't willing to say, and to find solutions we would never have found on our own. He asked questions that cut to the heart of our hopes and fears, and he found a path forward that was very workable. He said things to my dad that I wanted to say but didn't know how to say without a bomb going off, and He said things to me that my dad wanted to tell me but didn't know how to say. He made sure we put our agreement and our process on paper so misunderstandings would be minimized. I could easily see that if he hadn't done that, Dad and I would have had superficial conversations, thought we had come to agreement, but had missed each other on some crucial issues. When those things inevitably hit a snag, we probably would have felt betrayed, and hurt would have spiraled out of control.

As a crucial step, Dr. Chand told my dad to meet with the staff team to share the decision and the plans for the transition. He told Dad, "The transition can't happen until you tell them you're giving it your stamp of approval."

Dad changed the subject a bit: "I've been working with this staff for a really long time, and I love them very much. Is it okay if I go to staff meetings from time to time?"

I hoped he wasn't asking me. Thankfully, Dr. Chand stepped in. "No, after you tell them about the decision and thank them for serving, that's the last time you'll go to a staff meeting—unless Scott invites you to come." He must have seen the look of disappointment (and disagreement) on my dad's face because he quickly followed with, "And that's the way it has to be."

Dad came to a staff meeting, and he thanked them for serving with him to see God do amazing things. Dad told them, "Scott is your leader now, your only lead pastor. I know you'll follow the Lord and Scott with your whole heart. I'll pray for you, and I love you."

I asked all the staff to gather around Dad, and we all hugged him and prayed for him. I told him how grateful we were for all that he had done and how he had led the church. And I thanked him for his heart to educate children and lead Life School and for trusting God's call on my life.

For the next two years, when Dr. Chand visited our church, he met separately with me and my dad. He continued to be the mediator long after the actual transition took place. Why? Because perceptions, suspicions, and emotions didn't suddenly evaporate on the day the organizational chart changed. Both of us needed help to cope with the expectations of our new roles . . . and our expectations of each other. His input was invaluable.

Chapter 6

A Gift from God

Fifteen years after I sat in John Maxwell's office, humiliated because I had unknowingly become one of his illustrations, I was walking into my office on a normal Monday morning. My phone rang. It was Brett Eastman. He's a legend in the church world because he has produced popular video curriculum used in small groups in almost every church in America. I asked, "Hey, I haven't talked to you in a while. How are you doing?"

He replied, "Man, I'm in trouble! I need your help."

When people tell me they're "in trouble," I've learned to expect the worst. Instantly, my mind was racing: *What was going on with Brett? What was so bad that he'd call me, of all people?*

He explained, "We're doing John Maxwell's first video curriculum in a decade."

"That's cool!" I hadn't heard about any trouble so far. "What is it about?"

"It's called *Today Matters.*"

"I can't wait to see that. It'll be terrific!"

"Well," he told me, "you might be one of the first ones to see it. One of the three people scheduled to be on the panel had an emergency at his church, and he can't make it. Our video shoot is Wednesday." Now, I understood more about Brett's trouble, but I didn't see how I could help.

"John didn't know who could replace him, but I said, 'I think I know the right person.'"

I asked, "Really? Who is that?"

"You."

I reacted, "But John doesn't even know who I am!"

"Yeah, but I do, and I'm sure you'll do a great job. I told John about you, and he asked me to call you. If you can come, we'll fly you to Atlanta tomorrow, so you'll be ready Wednesday morning for the shoot." He paused for a few seconds to see if I wanted to say anything. I didn't. I was stunned. Brett continued, "I'll send you all the questions for the panel, so you'll be ready."

I told him, "Brett, I'd love to do this. It sounds amazing. I'm in. Send me the material, and I'll prepare."

He sounded like a ton had been lifted from his shoulders. "Thanks, Scott. You're saving my life."

As soon as the call ended, my son Hunter, who had been sitting there hearing the phone conversation, looked at me and asked, "Dad, you're going to be on a panel with John Maxwell?"

"Yeah, isn't that cool?"

"Cool? I'd be freaking out right now! Aren't you scared?"

I almost laughed. "Why would I be scared?"

Hunter knows me well. He looked at me like I'd lost my mind. "Dad, everything you know you learned from John Maxwell. You'll think everything you say is original, but everyone will know it sounds just like John! He'll say, 'Thanks, Scott. That was a really good point. I ought to know because I wrote it in one of my books.'"

I wanted to set the record straight: "Hunter, I know some stuff that didn't come from John."

"Are you sure?"

Hmmm. Actually, he was making a good point. I answered, "Well, I think I do."

After a few minutes, Hunter left, and I was alone with God. Confidence and joy soon were overshadowed by self-doubt. Did I answer too quickly? I didn't even pray about it! Instantly, I went back to the scene in Matthew 20. I sensed God ask me, *Scott, did you pick this seat on the panel? Did you manipulate anyone or anything to make it happen? Did you know it was happening? Did you try to promote yourself, so Brett would pick you?*

The answer to each question was undoubtedly, "No."

God assured me, *So you can be sure this is the seat I'm giving you. And if it's the seat I've chosen for you, you can be certain I've prepared you for it. I've made you ready for this seat on this panel at this time.*

When I landed in Atlanta, John's people picked me up and took me to a nice hotel. The next morning, they drove me to the studio. As I walked past the room where we would shoot the videos, I saw about fifty people who had flown in to be the audience. These weren't just folks; they were pastors and leaders from all over the country. I recognized many of them, which was a bit disconcerting. Who was I to be on a panel in front of them? I went back to the dressing area, and someone said, "Pastor Scott, it's time to put on your makeup."

Makeup? I'd never worn makeup in my life. I tried to convince him that I didn't need it, but he politely explained that the bright lights would cause a glare if I didn't have it on. After the medieval torture of having someone put makeup on me, Brett came in and escorted me to meet John.

He was so gracious. He said, "Thank you, Scott, for being on the panel with us today. You're saving the day. I'm really looking forward to interacting with you."

The four of us sat for the first session. John did a monologue, introduced us, and then began asking questions. When the first shoot was over, people in the audience applauded. I guess it wasn't too bad, huh?

Brett came to us and said, "That was the best thing we've ever done. Ever!"

John looked at us and gave us a thumbs-up.

After the second session, Brett told me, "Even better than the first one."

In the middle of the third one, after I answered a question, John stopped and said, "Wait a minute. Scott, say that again."

I said it again.

He reached over, gave me a high-five, and said, "Come on! Man, that's powerful!"

When the sixth and last session was over, everyone was very happy with how things had gone all day. Many of the people in the audience came up to shake our hands and thank us, and we thanked them for being so supportive.

A few minutes later, John asked me to join him in a nearby room. He asked Mark Cole, the president of John's companies, and Chad Johnson, his chief of staff, to join us.

John said, "I want to get a picture of this." Mark took out his phone to take a picture. John looked at me and said, "This has been a gift from God."

Mark said, "Absolutely. Today's shoot is a real gift."

John shook his head and smiled. He said, "I'm not talking about the video shoot. I'm talking about God sending Scott to be with us today. He's the gift from God." He hugged me, Mark took the picture, and then John told me, "I want to tell you this: God put us together today. I pray for winners to come into my life, and Scott, God has sent you." He paused for a few seconds and then said, "I can't say this to too many people, but I'm telling

Mark said, "Absolutely. Today's shoot is a real gift."

you: You came out for me today, and I'm going to come out for you. If I can ever serve you, preach for you, or open a door for you, I'd love to do it. And I believe God wants you to travel with me. I'm training leaders all over the world for national transformations. I'm going to Costa Rica in a few months. Would you consider going with me and being part of the team?"

I was very pleasantly surprised. I answered, "Certainly. I'd love to."

THE REALIZATION

Chad drove me to the airport, and on the way, he said, "Scott, today was amazing. It doesn't happen like this all the time. John was really impressed with you."

I got through security and boarded the plane to Dallas. When I sat down, I put my hands to my face to think about what had happened.

Then, it hit me: John had said exactly what I so desperately wanted him to say to me twenty-five years before at Prestonwood Baptist Church! I was so excited. I thanked the Lord for making the dream a reality, and I sensed Him reply, *Of course John said those things to you. This wasn't just your dream; it's Mine. But you weren't ready twenty-five years ago. Your motives hadn't been tested and purified. I've been working all these years to get your heart in the place it needs to be so you can handle the dream without it destroying you.*

My mind raced as I thought about the contrasts between then and now. As I prayed, God graciously showed me. When I was in my twenties:

- ◆ I wanted to be great.
- ◆ I tried to manipulate events to make things happen.
- ◆ I thought success was being famous.
- ◆ I was frantic and anxious.

But in my late forties:

- ◆ I want to be faithful.
- ◆ I trust God to make things happen.
- ◆ I've seen that success is being obedient to God.
- ◆ I have confidence that God is in control.

Over those years, God had reformed my motives, He had shown me that He's supremely trustworthy, and He had convinced me that He has my life in His hands.

GOD'S AUTHORITY, NOT MINE

Over the next few days, God led me to a passage in John's gospel. After Jesus healed the crippled man at the pool of Bethesda, the Jewish leaders were outraged that Jesus told the man to pick up his mat and walk. After all, it was the Sabbath, and they couldn't imagine God doing a miracle on His day. (They got things so wrong.) The leaders found Jesus and condemned Him. His answer probably confused them, but it made more sense to me than ever. He told them:

"Very truly I tell you, the Son can do nothing by himself; he can do only what he sees his Father doing, because whatever the Father does the Son also does. For the Father loves the Son and shows him all he does. Yes, and he will show him even greater works than these, so that you will be amazed." —John 5:19-20

If Jesus did only what His Father did, how ridiculous was it for me to try to make things happen on my own? Why did the Father reveal His will to Jesus? Because He loves Him. And what could Jesus expect? That the Father would do even greater miracles to astound everyone who saw them.

The difference between my twenties and forties is the realization that God is the King, and He's on His throne. He has called me to Himself, He has called me to a purpose, and He will fulfill that purpose as I trust Him. In fact, His love is so great that I can be sure He's more committed than I am to my accomplishing the purpose He's given me. Every day, I need to wake up and pray, "Lord, what do You want me

"Lord, what do You want me to say today? Where do You want me to go today? I'm Yours. Lead me, fill me, use me."

to say today? Where do You want me to go today? I'm Yours. Lead me, fill me, use me." The phone will ring when God causes it to ring. The invitation will come when I'm not seeking it or expecting it. The passage in Peter's first letter is familiar to us all, but it requires us to see that God's kingdom is upside down from the way the world works:

All of you, clothe yourselves with humility toward one another, because, "God opposes the proud but shows favor to the humble." Humble yourselves, therefore, under God's mighty hand, that he may lift you up in due time. Cast all your anxiety on him because he cares for you. —1 Peter 5:5-7

I sure don't want the God of the universe to oppose me! But I've learned (and I keep learning) that His special favor is toward those who come to Him with open hands and humble hearts, those who aren't into self-promotion or who attempt to control what God wants to do.

STILL IN THE OVEN

My dream wasn't dead; it was still baking in the oven for those twenty-five years. When I got home from John's talk at Prestonwood Baptist, I had been was confused and discouraged. I had no idea that there was any hope of the dream ever happening, but my hopelessness was a necessary part of the recipe. I had to give up on me making it happen and find peace with letting God do whatever He wanted to do. (It only took twenty-five years!)

When John said those kind words and invited me to join his team in Costa Rica, I was happy and thankful, but winning his favor had ceased to be the defining goal of my life. I could enjoy it without making it an idol that defined my identity.

THE PROCESS

When I told this story to a friend, he asked, "What would you say to people in their twenties, those in their forties, and even those in their sixties?"

I'd suspect that people in their twenties want, more than anything, for their lives to count, to do something great, to make a difference in the world. There's absolutely nothing wrong with zeal and idealism, but very few young people have had their motives tempered. I often think about my complaint to my dad when I was upset with God because He hadn't given me a dream comparable to Pastor Tommy Barnett's. Dad told me, "Just love God and love people. If you do those two things, God will give you everything you can handle."

I'd tell those young people, "God has a process for you. He'll develop you, deepen you, melt you, and mold you so you're prepared for what He calls you to be and do. Don't try to take shortcuts. They only lead to heartache and confusion. I ought to know."

The Bible tells us that when Joseph was young, he had two dreams about his parents and his brothers bowing down to him. He was so excited about the dreams that he couldn't wait to tell his family. But as you can imagine, his dad and brothers weren't that excited when they heard the part about them bowing down. In fact, they were quite offended.

The scenes in Joseph's early life help us understand what was happening. He was his dad's favorite, and everybody knew it. His brothers were working out in the fields tending livestock, but Joseph was hanging around his dad and enjoying the special gift of a beautiful coat. Then, his dad sent him out to check on his brothers—which was one of the dumbest parental decisions ever made! Didn't he know he was pouring gas on the brothers' fire of jealousy? I can imagine Joseph's superior attitude when he found them. But before he got close, they already had a plan to kill him.

His dreams were from God, but he wasn't ready to fulfill them. At this point in his life, he was a mama's boy and a daddy's boy. He was somewhat less than diplomatic to tell the whole family about his dream of ruling over them! And he didn't exactly have the greatest work ethic. Someday, Joseph would become one of the greatest leaders in history, but at this time, he was just a brat. He expected to be great, but he had no idea the process of fulfilling this dream would involve betrayal, slavery, and many years in an Egyptian prison. When God's timing was right, he was ready. Not before.

We begin to see character change in Joseph when he was sold as a slave to Potiphar, one of Pharaoh's officials. He was so gifted in administrating the household that Potiphar put him in charge of everything. Potiphar's wife took that to mean *everything*! When Joseph refused her seduction attempts, she accused him of attempted rape. Potiphar must have known the truth because Joseph surely would have been executed if he were really guilty. Instead, he was shipped off to prison. There, he proved again to be so gifted that he was put in charge of the prison. The inmate was running the jail! He had been betrayed by his brothers, enslaved in a foreign land, falsely accused of rape, and locked away with no hope of release. Others had abandoned him, but God was still faithful.

Through a series of God-orchestrated events, Joseph was put before Pharaoh to interpret a disturbing dream. (He was pretty good at dreams, if you remember.) He explained the meaning, and Pharaoh was so impressed that he made Joseph the prime minister of the nation, overseeing the harvest and storage of grain during seven years of bountiful harvest, so the people could survive the following seven years of famine. Success is where preparation and opportunity meet, and this was that moment in Joseph's life.

Hundreds of miles away in Palestine, Jacob and his family suffered in the famine. When Joseph's brothers arrived in Egypt to buy food, they had no idea that the official standing across from them was their own brother. Joseph didn't reveal his identity; instead, he shrewdly tested them to see if they would betray another brother to save their own skins. When they passed the test, he told them who he was. They were astounded. Pharaoh invited Jacob and his family to live in Egypt where Joseph could provide for their needs.

In this season of Joseph's life, we see a remarkable transformation: now the dream wasn't about him at all—it was about saving his family from starvation. It wasn't about his glorious future—it was about their future safety and nourishment. It wasn't about people bowing down to him—it was about him using his authority to care for his family and the nation. And because he served so well, God's people—and God's plan to bless the world through them—survived. We are the recipients of generation after generation of blessing, but it could have ended right there. The famine was a choke point that could have stopped it all, but God changed a brat into a humble and gifted man He could use to save the day and the people . . . and fulfill His ultimate purpose.

God sent Joseph through a grueling process, but it was necessary. When their father Jacob died, the brothers believed Joseph would exact revenge on them. They were scared. "His brothers then came and threw themselves down before him. 'We are your slaves,' they said" (Genesis 50:18).

Joseph assured them,

"Don't be afraid. Am I in the place of God? You intended to harm me, but God intended it for good to accomplish what is now being done, the saving of many lives. So then, don't be afraid. I will provide for you and your children." —Genesis 50:19-21

The dream was fulfilled: the brothers bowed down to Joseph. It was the same dream, but Joseph wasn't the same man. God had used those cruel years to soften his heart and give him patience with the process. Before, he had been enamored with his fame and his position, but now he realized God had put him in a position to save them. No one—not Joseph, not his father, and not his brothers—would have guessed that God would fulfill the dream in such a dramatic and surprising way to save his family.

I'd tell young people, "I appreciate your passion to make a difference, but don't be surprised when God shows you that your motives are an alloy of good and bad, both noble and selfish. Devote yourself to God, and experience His grace more than ever. With better motives, serve with no strings attached. Every day, wake up and ask God what He wants you to be, where He wants you to go, and what He wants you to say. Be faithful, and let Him measure your success."

People in their forties often look around to compare their lives with their peers. If they're in the top ranks, they feel good about themselves. If they're lower than the people around them, they either wilt and give up, redouble their efforts to rise in the pecking order, or find someone to blame. As long as our eyes are on other people, the only possible results are pride or shame. These feelings should be a red flag.

By the time we're in our forties, we may have more perception about our true motives, or on the other hand, we may be more blinded than ever to what's going on in our hearts. We need to get a good grasp of a kingdom perspective: The way up is down. The way to gain power is to give it away. The way to true riches is radical generosity. The last shall be first and the first shall be last. The greatest is the servant of all. This is at the heart of God's calling—for all of us, no matter our title or role.

In our forties, we may gain valuable insights about the process God has used to refine us and shape us. We see that God has had His hand on us even when we thought He'd left us high and dry. Gradually, we develop more confidence in His sovereign leadership in our lives, and we're confident He knows best. Trust crowds out worry.

Those in their sixties are often either deeply grateful or deeply discouraged. They look back at their lives and see the consequences of their choices, good or bad. They see how they trusted God, and He came through, or how they pursued their own agendas and ignored God's whispers. When I'm in my sixties, I want to look around and see spiritual sons and daughters who have sons and daughters who have sons and daughters.

We may think the prime of life is our forties and fifties, but if we've invested ourselves in raising up people who love God and love people with all their hearts, and they multiply in the lives of their own children—natural and spiritual—we'll be increasingly thrilled until our last day on earth. We'll be grateful for the things God has led us to do and the success we've had, but our greatest joy is knowing that our impact isn't over when we close our eyes for the last time. The generation after us will have the same heart and the same vision to raise up men and women who are sold out to God.

I've talked to countless men and women, from leaders in the church to those who are new believers, whose vision of success hasn't shifted beyond their own reputations. They want greatness or comfort or wealth or power or pleasure, and they haven't realized that those things can never really satisfy. Investing in others is the heartbeat of God. That's the message of the gospel: God invested His Son in saving those who didn't deserve it, and He continues to invest Himself in those who trust in Him. We gain by giving away. We rise by stooping to serve. We plant seeds of love, so other people can grow strong.

> **The generation after us will have the same heart and the same vision to raise up men and women who are sold out to God.**

In my twenties, it was all about me. In my forties, I learned that God's purposes and His path are far greater than anything I could have imagined. In my sixties, I expect to see the fruit of my love for many natural and spiritual sons and daughters.

When I'm old, I want to have a legacy like Jacob's. He, too, was a complicated man! As a young man, he and his mother had conspired to steal the birthright from his brother, Esau, but God met him one night and humbled him. After Joseph rose to power in Egypt, Jacob took his whole family to live there. Before he died, he gathered them all and blessed each son and their kids. He lived to see his sons and his grandchildren prosper. That's exactly what I want my legacy to be.

Chapter 7

Cutting Ties

It appears that God has kept me in "school" majoring in the same subject for the entirety of my life. Maybe I'm a slow learner, or maybe God knows this is the root issue of my heart. Negatively defined, it's the orphan mindset I described earlier: believing I never have enough, no one is looking out for me, I have to push and shove to find a place, feeling pressured to get attention and be promoted, living with what one pastor calls "radical insecurity," always checking out where I stand compared to others, reliving conversations because I'm sure I said something wrong or could have said it better, and experiencing high levels of anxiety as my daily routine. Defined positively, God's course load is about grasping the wonder that the infinitely powerful God is also infinitely loving . . . toward me! I'm a child of the King, deeply loved, completely forgiven, and totally accepted—not because of my performance, but apart from it—or more accurately, in spite of it. It's all about grace. As my heavenly Father, He knows what's best for me, He knows the right path for me, He knows the right timing for me . . . so I can relax and trust Him.

Over the years, the curriculum escalated from lessons equivalent to arithmetic, then fractions, geometry, trigonometry, and finally, differential calculus. Each level was quite a challenge—I'm not that great at math! And from my struggles, it's obvious that I haven't been that great at trusting the Father's heart and His hand on my life.

THREE CORDS

A few months after I was on the panel with John in Atlanta, God put me on the front row for my next course. One night, I woke up at 3 a.m. I could tell this wasn't just a bathroom trip or a sudden bout of hunger. God wanted to speak to me. I walked upstairs to be alone with Him. I paced the floor like I often do when I pray. I said, "God, speak to me. What do You want to say to me?"

At that moment, I had a vision of three men standing around me just a few feet away. I didn't have to wonder who they were. It was clear. They were Justin Lathrop, Sam Chand, and Rob Ketterling—three men who have meant the world to me and have been incredible resources. At the time, all three of them were serving positionally as overseers for me and Oaks Church. In the vision, there were three strands coming out of my soul, one connected to each of them. I prayed, "Lord, what are You saying?"

I sensed Him say, *Do you see Justin? He's your promotion. Every time you write a book, every time you need to hire a staff member, every time you want to speak somewhere, every time you want to meet a leader you admire, and every time you want someone to promote your interests, you call Justin. I've gifted him to promote people and organizations. That's his calling in the kingdom, but there's a problem: you call him before you call*

Me. I'm through sharing your highest loyalty with Justin. Either I'm your promotion or he is. It's up to you.

I responded, "Okay, I understand. I've made Justin an idol, and I've looked to him instead of You. God, You're my promotion, not Justin. I love Justin, but as of right now, I no longer depend on him for my promotion. In the name of Jesus, I cut the cord between him and me." With a wave of my hand, I cut the cord with Justin.

I sensed the Lord direct me to look at Dr. Chand. God said to me, *Do you see Dr. Chand? He's your protection. Every time you have a problem with your board, every time there's a difficult situation with one of your staff members, and every time you're confused because you don't know how to do something, you call him before you ask Me for help. I've gifted him to help leaders with problems and opportunities, and I brought him into your life, but you're looking to him instead of Me. Aren't you aware that I know infinitely more than he does about what's going on and what's best for you? Don't you know that I have far more wisdom than he does? Which do you want, infinite wisdom and love or finite wisdom and love? I'm through sharing you with Dr. Chand. You can either have him as your protection or Me. It's up to you.*

I answered, "God, as much as I appreciate Dr. Chand, he can't compare with You. You're my protection. In the name of Jesus, I cut the cord of idolatry with Dr. Chand." And with a stroke of my hand, the cord was cut and fell away.

I sensed God say, *Do you see Rob? You've made him your primary source of provision.*

I pushed back, "Lord, I've never asked him for a dollar!"

Yes, God explained, *but you asked him to be an overseer, so you could learn how he raises money for his church and missions. You've trusted him to take you to the next level in financing growth. You need to know, I've gifted him for that, but I know your people far better than Rob does. I know their businesses, their incomes, and their hearts. I'm the one who speaks to them to unlock their generosity. Rob can't do that. I'm the one who can bless their businesses. I'm the one who opens the floodgates of heaven to pour out blessings on them, so they want to give more. You have a choice: you can trust Rob to be your provision, or you can trust Me. It's your choice. Which do you want?*

Instantly I responded, "Oh, Lord, You know I want You! You are my provision. In the name of Jesus, I cut the cord between Rob and me." I waved my hand to cut the cord, and it was severed.

At that moment, I felt such profound relief and joy. God had spoken. He'd revealed a barrier between Him and me (actually, three barriers), and He'd graciously invited me to respond in faith. I raised my fists to heaven, not in defiance, but in faith. I said, "God, You know that I don't have what it takes. I don't have the wisdom, I don't have the power, and I don't have the authority to lead our church the way You want me to. I'm

> **At that moment, I felt such profound relief and joy. God had spoken. He'd revealed a barrier between Him and me (actually, three barriers), and He'd graciously invited me to respond in faith.**

so sorry. Justin isn't my promotion; You are. Dr. Chand isn't my protection; You are. Rob isn't my provision; You are." I opened my hands and said, "I give it all to You, Lord. I declare that You are my everything. I'm

Yours—completely. I trust in You, Father. You will take care of me in Your perfect way in Your perfect timing. I step down from the throne of my heart, and I ask You to take that seat. You are my King. I'll go where You want me to go. I'll say what You want me to say. And I'll do what You want me to do. You are my promotion, my protection, and my provision. I trust in You."

I got on my knees before my Lord the King. For a while, it was right to just be quiet and let the moment sink in. But God wasn't quite through with me that night. I sensed Him say, *Okay, now you need to go to each one to tell them about your decision tonight.*

I thought of a dozen reasons why this wasn't a good idea, but before I could voice any of them, God said, *You need to explain your new commitments and assure them it's not because they've done anything wrong. It's because you trusted them more than Me. It's your problem; not theirs. And there's another step: because it would be easy for you to trust them too much again, you need to release them from being overseers.*

I reacted, "God, that's so embarrassing! And besides, they'll think this is just some lame excuse to get them to stop being overseers. What'll they think when I say, 'God told me all this'?"

The Lord's response wasn't exactly eloquent, but it was clear: *Just do it.*

A NOT-VERY-SUBTLE PROD
I went back to bed. The next day, I flew to Pittsburg to be part of a Church Multiplication Network event. After it ended, I was in the airport with Scott Hagan, waiting to board my flight back to Dallas. He was also involved in the CMN conference. He's a dear friend and a powerful man of prayer. Out of the blue, he turned to me and said, "Umm, Scott,

I feel prompted to tell you something. I have no idea why, but it's clear to me that I need to say it."

I said, "Go for it."

"Well," he began, "I've been studying the life of Moses, and I believe God wants me to tell you about a particular moment. Scott, what do you think was the scariest moment in Moses' life?"

"Standing at the Red Sea with Pharaoh's army about to attack and nowhere to run?"

"Maybe, but I don't think so. It was an event that happened between the burning bush, when God commanded Moses to go back to Egypt to free His people, and when he actually stood before Pharaoh. In the light of the burning bush, God told him, 'Tell them *I AM* has sent you. I have your back. I'll do miracle after miracle to show that I'm with you. This isn't your idea. I picked you for this task.'"

I was listening. I had no clue how all this fit into what God wanted to say to me, but I had no doubt that it did.

Scott continued, "Moses gave excuses why he wasn't qualified, but God told him, 'Am I not the one who made you? I know who you are and where you've been. And I know how I've prepared you for this great task. I've called you, and I'll make you successful.'"

Still listening. . . .

"Moses went back to his house, packed up his wife and kids, and started the trip to Egypt. On the way, God got so angry with Moses that He wanted to kill him! Why? We don't know exactly. In a very strange passage, we see that Zipporah, Moses' wife, grabbed a knife to circumcise their son. When she was done, she threw the foreskin at Moses and told him, 'You're a bloody husband!' At that moment, God's anger faded away. I'm not sure exactly what's going on here, but we know this:

God was angry because Moses considered something very important to God to be trivial. God wanted Moses to be ready to meet Pharaoh ... completely consecrated and totally submitted. Circumcising his son was a crucial part of Moses' consecration, but he didn't believe it was very important. Circumcision was the sign of the covenant between God and His people. It meant that God's people were cutting away anything of the world, so they could be completely devoted to Him. Cutting the foreskin was a sign of cutting the cord with the world."

Scott stopped for a few seconds, and then he told me, "I don't know why I'm telling you all this, but I think something's going on with you like it was going on with Moses. God is calling you to something greater than ever. If you're going to rise to a new level of leadership, you have to go to a new depth of commitment. What was okay in the past is no longer okay with God. Scott, I think you're going to have to cut some things out, so you can follow God with your whole heart."

I'm not sure when it dawned on me that God was speaking through my friend, but near the end, I was shaking. "Cutting." Scott's repeated use of the word wasn't a coincidence. I knew God was telling me that He was serious about my cutting ties with Justin, Dr. Chand, and Rob. I told Scott about waking up in the middle of the night and God giving me a vision of the three men. I explained my conversation with God, cutting the cords, and His instruction to call them.

Scott could tell I was afraid of something, so he jumped in: "Bro, I know these guys. They're not going to misunderstand. They'll get it. Are you afraid they'll think you've lost your mind? They won't. Do you think they'll see it as odd that God spoke to you, and you're being obedient to Him? No way. They'll be completely supportive." He stopped for a second, and then he added, "You've got to make the calls. If you don't, what does that say about you?"

Ouch. Scott's bold challenge was unsettling, but Proverbs says that "wounds from a friend can be trusted" (Proverbs 27:6). Scott was a true friend at that moment.

A few minutes later, it was time for me to board the plane. When I found my seat, I put my face in my hands, just like I'd done a few months before, after being on the panel with John. I prayed. I cut the ties again, and I reaffirmed my full surrender to the Father. As I prayed, I went to the passage in Exodus 4, and I began writing as God revealed some applications from the story of Moses and Zipporah.

> **I prayed. I cut the ties again, and I reaffirmed my full surrender to the Father.**

At that pivotal moment, God had called Moses to confront the most powerful leader in the most powerful nation on earth. It's no wonder he was reluctant. He had a lot to overcome. I realized that Moses was an orphan. His mother had to give him up to save his life. He was adopted by Pharaoh's daughter. He grew up in splendor, but he suffered from insecurities. He was adopted, he was different, and he wasn't an insider, so he developed an orphan mindset. He tried to take things into his own hands by killing an Egyptian, and then he ran for his life.

In Midian, he thought caring for sheep was the best life he could expect. His dreams of greatness had been shattered long ago. When God appeared to him in the burning bush, Moses didn't have the self-confidence to say, "Yes, I'll do it." When he was finally convinced it was God's will for him (and Aaron) to demand freedom for God's people, he started moving toward Egypt. Forty years of tending sheep had humbled Moses, but he wasn't quite ready for his big moment. God had to purge him of doubts and hesitation. God had to bring him to a deeper point of dependence. The moment of his son's circumcision was crucial. Moses wouldn't have been able to stand the pressure of the confrontations with Pharaoh if he hadn't fully surrendered to God.

After thinking about all of this, I sensed God say, *Scott, this is what I'm doing in you. You can't fulfill what I'm calling you to be and do without being fully surrendered and dependent on Me. For years, your dependence on Justin, Dr. Chand, and Rob didn't significantly stop you from being what I want you to be, but it does now. I'm calling you to something bigger, and it's time to deal with anything and everything that's in the way. That's what I did with Moses, and that's what I'm doing with you. I'm calling you to a new level of covenant and commitment. You'll need to be at this level because the pressures are going to be greater than ever. But you're ready. I've prepared you. Depend on Me.*

As the plane took off, I made a commitment to call Justin, Dr. Chand, and Rob in the coming week.

Before each call, I swallowed hard and punched in the number. I told each of them the story of God speaking to me in the night, the vision of cutting the cords, and Scott Hagan relating the obscure story of the circumcision of Moses' son. I explained, "I'm not cutting our friendship, but I have to cut my dependence on you. As an act of obedience, I'm not going to call you unless God directs me to call you. If you take the initiative with me, that's fine, but I can't take the initiative with you. I'm convinced God brought you into my life, but in this season, I need to be sure I trust in God instead of depending primarily on you. I hope you understand."

They were very gracious. They didn't say, "Man, you've lost your mind!" Each of them expressed confidence that this realization and the new commitment were good and right . . . and sovereignly directed by God.

At that time, I had no idea what my pharaoh might be. I didn't know what God was preparing me to be and do, but I wanted to be ready. In the weeks that followed, I often thought about the story in Exodus 4. I wasn't afraid that God was so angry that He wanted to kill me; I was afraid I'd miss the opportunity for Him to use me.

DAILY DECLARATION

I know myself fairly well. I'm a drifter. If I don't nail down what God is teaching me, I drift back into the same old thoughts and habits. Like a schoolboy learning his multiplication tables, I need repetition to learn my lessons. I've often thought about the night God gave me the vision of my three friends and my response to Him.

As an act of faith and commitment, every morning I make the same declaration I made that night. I raise my fists over my head and say, "Father, I don't have it. I don't have the strength, wisdom, or authority to lead my life the way You can. I step down from the throne of my heart and invite You to take that seat. I submit to Your rule and reign. You are my sovereign Lord, my Life, my King." Then I open my hands in a "kingdom victory stance" and pray, "Father, I surrender everything I am and everything I have to You. I will go where You want me to go, I'll say what You want me to say, and I'll do what You want me to do. I trust in You. You are my promotion, my protection, and my provision."

HOW CAN YOU TELL?

When I told this story, a friend asked, "Scott, how can you tell when you're trusting in people more than God? What are the signs?"

I responded, "For me, at least, it's all about the order of my dependence. Is my first inclination to go to someone or to go to God? Do I pick up the phone, or do I take time to pray first? There's absolutely nothing wrong with getting advice from people we trust, but do we trust them more than we trust God?"

Idolatry may not mean we completely reject one god and replace it with another. It may mean that we put our resources—and our dependence on those resources—in the wrong order. We usually think of sin as behavior that's destructive to us and others. It's that, but it's more than that. Sixteen centuries ago, Augustine said our problem is "disordered loves," that is, we love secondary things as if they're primary, and we love primary things as if they're secondary. How can we tell? By examining our worries. What are we afraid of losing? What daydreams and nightmares are recurring? But it's not just worry. Our most profound emotions—fear, despair, resentment, shame, and anxiety, for starters—give us a glimpse into what really matters to us.

I'd like to say that we can just ask ourselves, "Is anything more important to me than God?" But most of us aren't that self-perceptive. God has to break in, jolt us awake, and give us a blast of insight that we didn't have before. Thankfully, God doesn't blast us when we put prestige, possessions, or power in His rightful place on the throne of our lives. If He did, none of us would be around. What I'm trying to say is that to some degree, all of us are guilty of idolatry, and none of us has pure motives. The wise and mature among us can admit that we have idols, and we're not surprised when God shines a light on even more of them (or bigger ones of the same sort we thought we'd already conquered). When they're exposed—like God revealed my dependence on Justin, Dr. Chand, and Rob—we can repent and put God where He is supposed to be: on the throne . . . reigning, ruling, loving, and leading.

Why was it so easy for me to depend on these men? I can identify several reasons: They're tangible; I didn't have to wonder if they'd respond to me. They're gifted, and they have a proven track record. Depending on them was the easiest thing in the world. To be sure, they played a crucial role in an important season of my life. I wouldn't have grown, and our church wouldn't have grown, without their influence. But I trusted them more than I trusted God.

> **Thankfully, God doesn't blast us when we put prestige, possessions, or power in His rightful place on the throne of our lives. If He did, none of us would be around.**

The next season required dramatic action to cut the ties that bound my heart to these men. They're still dear friends, and I treasure them, but I've made a point to treasure Jesus more.

God called Moses before he obeyed and before his son was circumcised, and God was calling me to address my misplaced dependence before He showed me the next season. His calling preceded my preparation, and my obedience preceded God's revelation of the exact nature of the calling.

God didn't take Moses through the path of consecration because He was angry with him. He put him on his path because He knew Moses would rise to the calling. In the same way, God didn't appear to me in the vision that night because He was furious with me. It was part of the journey to prepare me for the next season of usefulness. I believe God was saying, "A higher level of calling brings a higher level of intimidation, temptation, and challenge. You need a higher level of dependence on Me, so you can stand strong."

Let me be very clear: I am saying that all of us have a tendency to treasure approval, power, wealth, comfort, and pleasure more than God. But I'm not saying that when God shows us these disordered loves, we need to cut those people and things out of our lives. We certainly need to make a heart adjustment, and we need to tell somebody about our decision. But we may not (and probably won't) need to call those people and change a leadership structure around us. I had to do that because those men were overseers, and I needed to have them step away from having authority over me—entirely for my sake, not because of any flaw in them—and I needed to do something that would be a clear line in the sand in my progress of sanctification and consecration.

You may not need to tell the people about your spiritual decision when you cut ties and remove them from the throne of your heart, but you need to tell somebody. Talk to your spouse, a close friend, a mentor, or counselor. If you verbalize your act of repentance and commitment, it will become stronger. If you don't tell anyone, it'll be very easy to slip back into the same idolatrous thoughts, feelings, and habits.

All of us need to set good limits and boundaries. Limits are how far I'm willing to go in a relationship. In this case, it means I make sure I'm not operating out of a savior complex. I trust God to work in people's lives, and I ask Him for direction, so I don't step over the line. Boundaries are how far I'm willing to let other people go in their relationship to me. I don't let them tell me God's will, I don't depend on them for what only God can give, and I don't let them sit on the throne of my heart.

These are insights and decisions I make every day. I have to set limits on my involvement in my sons' lives, so I let them make their own decisions. They're adults. If they want my advice, I need to let them ask for it. (Pardon me while I put a new bandage on my tongue. I've had to bite it too often!) And I make decisions about boundaries. I value God's design and His input more than anyone else's—at least, that's my commitment. When people tell me they know what's best for me, I don't just jump to do what they suggest or insist. I listen, I pray, and I trust God to give me wisdom.

I've taught the first verses of Romans 12 so often that I've lost count, but after God gave me the vision of the three men and asked me to cut the cords of dependence on them, the passage has taken on a deeper meaning. Paul wrote,

> *Therefore, I urge you, brothers and sisters, in view of God's mercy, to offer your bodies as a living sacrifice, holy and pleasing to God—this is your true and proper worship. Do not conform to the pattern of this world, but be transformed by the renewing of your mind. Then you will be able to test and approve what God's will is—his good, pleasing and perfect will. —Romans 12:1-2*

Our dedication to put God first is a response to His amazing grace, not a Pharisaic duty. When His love captures our hearts, we realize He has given everything to us, so we give everything to Him. He's "the first giver." But even then, the lure of the world is strong, and the fight of renewal is ongoing. Devotion pleases Him, and it's the only way for us to thrive.

Cut the ties that bind you to secondary things. It's the path to freedom, peace, power, and usefulness. It's the only way to reach the potential of being who God has created you to be. Isn't that what you really want?

Chapter 8

Growing Up, Stepping Out

My dad instilled in me a passionate desire to learn and grow. From my earliest childhood, our family read together, and my dad spent a lot of time telling stories. From him, I learned that a wide world of knowledge was readily available. When Dad opened his cabinet and showed me the hundreds of John Maxwell cassette tapes, he fired the booster rocket in my desire to grow. As I listened to five of those messages every week and spoke on one of them, John's biblical and practical concepts became deeply ingrained in my heart and mind.

In my thirties, I read a book a week, usually about leadership. In my forties, I began listening to podcasts of the very best communicators, I kept reading, I attended conferences, and Dr. Chand gave me plenty of steps to take in my development. At his suggestion, I started seeing a gifted counselor, and I found a financial adviser. I realized I needed to fight against middle-age spread, so I got into a CrossFit exercise program. I hadn't started out to create a "growth team," but that's what happened.

After the vision about Justin, Dr. Chand, and Rob, and my calls to them, I believed God had prepared me for something really great. I was ready! But that's not what happened. Instead, I entered a period of spiritual and emotional drought. As the months went by, I felt stagnant. My upward trajectory lost power, and I wasn't sure what was blocking my progress.

John had asked me to go with him to Costa Rica as part of his team. Even though I felt like I was going backward, I was glad to go. While we were there, he spoke to leaders in government and business. One day he asked me to sit with him during a live radio interview. Somewhere in the middle of the program, the host asked him, "How important is self-image?"

John responded immediately, "Oh, it's tremendously important. It's the lid to your personal growth."

As soon as the words came out of his mouth, it hit me: I'd read hundreds of books (including all of John's), I'd listened to thousands of tapes and podcasts, and I had enlisted a team of people to help me grow, but somehow, I'd missed this crucial point: My self-concept was the lid to my personal growth. In other words, I can't grow beyond how I see myself. "The Law of the Lid" tells us that leadership ability is the lid that determines a person's level of effectiveness. An organization cannot grow beyond the leadership ability of the leader. But the "Law of the Lid" also applies to the limitations a poor self-image can put on our personal growth.

When I got back home, I devoured books and podcasts about a gospel-centered self-image. In my study, I kept coming back to the story of David. We often think of David as the young man who killed the giant, Goliath, or the great king who united God's people into one nation, but his story is more complex and interesting. We first see David—or actually, we don't see him, which is part of the story—when God sends Samuel to Bethlehem to the house of Jesse to anoint one of his sons to replace the inept King Saul. When Samuel arrived, he told the elders of the city to invite "Jesse and his sons" to a special sacrifice. When they arrived, Samuel looked at Eliab and concluded, "Surely the Lord's anointed stands here before the Lord." But the Lord told him, "Do not consider his appearance or his height, for I have rejected him. The Lord does not look at the things people look at. People look at the outward appearance, but the Lord looks at the heart."

One by one, Jesse brought his seven sons to stand before Samuel, but the prophet told him, "The Lord has not chosen these." Samuel must have been perplexed. How could he choose one of Jesse's sons if the Lord said "no" to all of them? He asked Jesse, "Are these all the sons you have?"

"There is still the youngest," Jesse answered. "He is tending the sheep."

When David came in from the pasture, the Lord told Samuel, "Rise and anoint him; this is the one." The historian tells us: "So Samuel took the horn of oil and anointed him in the presence of his brothers, and from that day on the Spirit of the Lord came powerfully upon David. Samuel then went to Ramah" (1 Samuel 16:5-13).

The message was clear: David's dad didn't consider him important enough to be included in "all his sons." It's my guess that this wasn't the only time Jesse devalued his youngest son, and it's my guess that the brothers followed their dad's example and despised their little brother. Samuel had come to give Jesse a great honor of anointing one of his sons as the new king, but Jesse didn't consider David to be king material. In fact, he didn't even consider him to be son material. And where was David's mom? Why didn't she speak up for him and defend him? We hear only silence.

Put yourself in the story. What messages did David absorb every day? "You're worthless." "You don't count." "We don't need you, and in fact, we don't want you!" David had a deep sense of emotional abandonment and abuse. He described the inner turmoil in Psalm 69:

For I endure scorn for your sake, and shame covers my face. I am a foreigner to my own family, a stranger to my own mother's children . . . You know how I am scorned, disgraced and shamed; all my enemies are before you. Scorn has broken my heart and has left me helpless; I looked for sympathy, but there was none, for comforters, but I found none. —Psalm 69:7-8, 19-20

In another psalm, we get another glimpse of the relational trauma David endured, but here, we also see where he found a new sense of identity: "Though my father and mother forsake me, the Lord will receive me" (Psalm 27:10). The healing of his heart may have begun when Samuel poured the anointing oil on his head in front of his parents, his brothers, the city elders, and anyone else who was there. Oil is a symbol of the Holy Spirit. It wasn't dabbed on; it was poured from a horn. If we'd been there, we would have seen the oil flow down his head where his thoughts needed to be touched by the Spirit. We'd have seen it drip off his ears where he needed God's affirming messages to replace the toxic words he'd been hearing all his life. We'd see it cover his eyes, so he could begin to see himself more clearly from God's perspective. We'd see it on his lips where he would begin to speak of God's glory and grace and lead with wisdom and power. Finally, it would flow down onto his clothes and cover his heart where God's healing was beginning and where his motives would line up with God's. David's family may have said, "You're a nobody!" But God was saying, "You're special to Me. I love you. I have big plans for you, and I'll be with you every step of the way."

I can almost hear God tell David, "Your dad may not consider you part of the family, and your brothers think you're a loser, but you're the one I've chosen to be the shepherd-king of My people." God's confirmation happened "in the presence of his brothers" and the others who were watching. And at that moment, "the Spirit of the Lord came powerfully upon David." The inner transformation began at the very

> **But God was saying, "You're special to Me. I love you. I have big plans for you, and I'll be with you every step of the way."**

place of David's deepest wound and the lies his father and brothers said about him.

David was changed, but his family members weren't. After anointing David, Samuel left. He was there for this pivotal moment in the history of God's people, and then he was gone. He didn't stick around to disciple David, he didn't get involved in family therapy, and he didn't engage in conflict resolution. He left David in the exact place where he'd been earlier that morning—in the home of people who didn't value him in the least. David had a choice: Would he be the person his brothers and his dad said he was, a shepherd boy who was an outcast with no future, or would he be the person God said he was, a shepherd of sheep who was destined to be the greatest king of God's people? This wasn't a one-time decision. Emotional healing doesn't happen like that. Many times every day, David had to soften his heart to hear God's tender message of love and purpose, and he had to steel himself to ward off the bitterness and lies of those who lived under the same roof with him.

STILL NOT WORTHY

We might think that having a powerful prophet come to the house and anoint their little brother would radically change the perspective of David's brothers, but it didn't. The next scene where we see them is in Saul's army post, listening to the taunts of the Philistine giant, Goliath. Three of Jesse's sons were soldiers. They cowered in fear with the rest of Saul's men as Goliath yelled threats day after day. One day Jesse sent David to the front to take grain, bread, and cheese to his brothers. When David arrived, he heard Goliath's roar.

David asked some men, "What will be done for the man who kills this Philistine and removes this disgrace from Israel? Who is this uncircumcised Philistine that he should defy the armies of the living God?" (1 Samuel 17:26) They told him the king promised riches, his daughter's hand in marriage, and tax exemption (it was attractive then, too!) to the man who killed the giant.

David's oldest brother Eliab overheard the conversation. He was irate and asked, "Why have you come down here? And with whom did you leave those few sheep in the wilderness? I know how conceited you are and how wicked your heart is; you came down only to watch the battle" (1 Samuel 17:28). In other words, "Who do you think you are? I don't care who anointed you, you're still a punk. You're still nothing. Give me the cheese and get out of here!"

When we read the Scriptures, we need to read in context. Many people read episodically, and they miss the deeper meanings. In this case, we often skip over an important period between Samuel's anointing David and David's killing Goliath. Where was David during that time? He was in Saul's palace! When the Spirit of the Lord came upon David, He departed from King Saul and was replaced by an evil spirit. The king was tormented, so his attendants recommended music therapy. Who could play the lyre beautifully? David. Can you imagine what was going on in David's head when messengers came to Bethlehem to ask him to come to the palace to play for the king? Jesse and the brothers must have been shocked at the honor . . . and the irony. While David was in the palace, playing the lyre to soothe Saul's troubled soul and watching the rest of the family and attendants, he knew God had chosen him to be the new king, but he wasn't in a hurry to make that announcement to a demon-possessed boss!

Back to the battlefield. . . . When David learned that Saul had promised riches and his daughter to anyone who could kill Goliath, it was no abstract offer. He had seen the riches of the king, and he had noticed the beauty of his daughters. David knew what the rewards would be if he killed the giant. You know the story. He went toward Goliath with a sling and five stones—no armor, just raw courage and the Spirit of the Lord. He killed the giant with a single shot and became the hero of the day!

After the battle, David became a leader of the army, and he succeeded in every mission. In fact, when people praised David more than Saul, the king's jealousy raged. Twice he tried to pin him to the wall with a spear—not exactly a happy, supportive environment for young David! It must have felt a lot like home.

It was time for Saul to make good on his promise. He told David, "Here is my older daughter Merab. I will give her to you in marriage; only serve me bravely and fight the battles of the Lord" (1 Samuel 18:17).

David didn't say, "Thanks," and marry Merab. Instead, he groveled: "Who am I, and what is my family or my clan in Israel, that I should become the king's son-in-law?" The historian tells us, "So when the time came for Merab, Saul's daughter, to be given to David, she was given in marriage to Adriel of Meholah" (1 Samuel 18:19).

What just happened? David had been anointed king by the famous prophet Samuel. He had been honored to play the lyre for the king. He had killed the giant and routed the Philistine army, and he had defeated many other enemies of the nation. Saul had promised Merab to him, but David still didn't believe he was worthy. This isn't humility; it's pride. Pride? Yeah, pride. Self-pity and self-denigration are the refusal to believe what God says about us. It's believing our self-evaluation is more accurate than God's, that we know more about ourselves than God does. When God says, "You're a king" but you say, "No, I'm not king material," that's trusting yourself more than you trust God, which is a form of pride. Self-pity is pride turned inside out.

David was still insecure even after Samuel anointed him, Goliath fell before him, armies were defeated by him, and Saul made promises to him. The lies of his father and his brothers were still more powerful in his self-perception than God's stamp of approval. He had been told that he didn't fit in his family, and now he believed he didn't fit in the palace. His low self-esteem effectively blocked his experience of God's blessings. Instead of the positive effects of the anointing oil, the sludge of self-pity blinded his eyes, stuffed his ears, caused him to speak words of self-doubt, and clouded his heart.

Each of us has a self-image bucket, and it has a hole at the level where we believe what God says about us. When we experience blessings above that line, it leaks down to that level. God's affirmation of David and the appreciation of the people was at a 9.9, but David still saw himself as a 3. So at this moment, he acted like a 3. How much are we like David? How much do we block God's blessings because we don't believe God has given us an identity that is based on the gospel truths of His love, forgiveness, and adoption as children of the King?

> **Each of us has a self-image bucket, and it has a hole at the level where we believe what God says about us. When we experience blessings above that line, it leaks down to that level.**

Where is the hole in your bucket?

PAUL'S PRAYER

In his book, *And David Perceived He Was King*, Pastor Dale Mast gives us this insight: "What David's faith could obtain, his identity could not contain."[3] He means there's often a difference between what we say we believe, our faith, and what defines our sense of who we are, our identity. That has certainly been true for me. I have preached hundreds of messages on the gospel of grace, Christ's unmerited favor for us, but I've realized that my identity has been shaped by more than Jesus. It was shaped by messages I internalized, my own innate selfishness and

3   Dale Mast, *And David Perceived He Was King* (Camarillo, CA: Xulon Elite, 2015), 175.

blindness, and experiences that created hurt, fear, and shame. Those "truths" seemed absolutely certain . . . bedrock beliefs that could never be shaken. But they can be, and they need to be, shaken. How can our sense of identity expand to contain all God wants for us?

We get a glimpse of the solution in Paul's second prayer in his letter to the Ephesians. He begins the letter talking about our identity in Christ: we're chosen, adopted, forgiven, and sealed by the Holy Spirit. He prays that God would open their eyes to see the true nature of their calling, the fact that he considers himself to be rich because we belong to Him, and the surpassing greatness of His power. He then launches into an explanation of the gospel, and he doesn't want us to miss that it's a free gift. He says that the gospel tears down walls of suspicion, resentment, and bitterness between races. How do we live all this out? How can all these truths sink so deep into our souls that they form our very identity? He knows we will only grasp all this with the help of the Lord, so he stops his teaching, gets on his knees, and starts praying:

For this reason I kneel before the Father, from whom every family in heaven and on earth derives its name. I pray that out of his glorious riches he may strengthen you with power through his Spirit in your inner being, so that Christ may dwell in your hearts through faith. And I pray that you, being rooted and established in love, may have power, together with all the Lord's holy people, to grasp how wide and long and high and deep is the love of Christ, and to know this love that surpasses knowledge—that you may be filled to the measure of all the fullness of God.

Now to him who is able to do immeasurably more than all we ask or imagine, according to his power that is at work within us, to him be glory in the church and in Christ Jesus throughout all generations, for ever and ever! Amen. —*Ephesians 3:14-21*

Let's take a closer look: Paul wasn't only praying for the Ephesians; he was praying for "all the Lord's holy people"—people like you and me. He asked God to make His love so real that we'd be rooted in it like a tall, strong tree and established on it like a solid building. He asked the Father to work His love so deeply in us that we'd grasp it in our inner being—our deepest thoughts, our self-perception, our sense of worth. When this is happening, we're "filled to the measure of all the fullness of God." Isn't that what you and I want more than anything? It's the experience of a love that consumes us, burns away the lies, heals the wounds, and fills us with the unutterable joy of the Lord. Then, and only then, will we reach the full potential of what God wants for us. Paul ended his prayer with an explosion of praise and a pointed request: that God would do more in us than we can possibly imagine, His power would be unleashed, we'd live for Him, and we'd have a powerful impact on generations to come.

If our self-image comes into alignment with who God says we are, and if we'll be humble enough to believe that we're more valuable to Him than the stars in the sky, we'll leave an inheritance of a secure identity to our children and grandchildren. We can't give away something we don't possess. We can't instill a gospel-shaped self-concept in others if we don't have it in us, and we can't take them to a place where we've never been. The most important step, then, is for you and me to pray Paul's prayer . . . and believe God when He speaks His love into our hearts.

SLOW, VERY SLOW

David struggled with his identity for years. He was a brilliant special ops commander as he led his "mighty men" against Saul's jealousy-driven attacks, he was a gifted political leader who united the nation, and he was a powerful army commander who won battle after battle. But for years, David didn't believe, in the depths of his heart, that he was really a delight to God. How do we know? The historian tells us,

> *Now Hiram king of Tyre sent envoys to David, along with cedar logs and carpenters and stonemasons, and they built a palace for David. Then David knew that the Lord had established him as king over Israel and had exalted his kingdom for the sake of his people Israel.* —2 Samuel 5:11-12

"Then David knew"—he only believed the truth of his identity as God's anointed king long after Samuel anointed him, he killed the giant, he won military victories, and he orchestrated the union of the tribes into the nation of Israel. He knew only when another king confirmed it. When David built a new palace with the lumber and stone provided by King Hiram, he could walk around every day seeing tangible proof that he was really the king.

In the same way, our presidents live in the White House. Some of them have had homes that are even more grand, but they live at 1600 Pennsylvania Avenue because they're the leaders of the entire country; they don't just represent themselves. The White House was built to reinforce the identity and dignity of the President of the United States, and each inhabitant, like David, has a constant reminder of his (or someday, her) identity. When the band plays "Hail to the Chief," that's not about the person; it's about the calling to be the leader of our great nation.

David finally came into agreement with God that he was the chosen king of Israel. God didn't choose him, so he could be powerful and famous but to serve the people with honor, wisdom, and justice. In the same way, your calling isn't primarily for you; it's for others. God has chosen you, He has called you, He has adopted you, and He has anointed and empowered you to serve the people in your home, your neighborhood, your school, your business, and your community. Everywhere you go, people need Jesus, and you are the voice, hands, and feet of Jesus in their lives.

If you're a mom or a dad, the greatest gift you can give your kids is to call out the greatness God has put in them. Your challenge is to see beyond the struggles of the day and look beneath their childishness to determine who God is creating them to become. Be like Samuel with David. Listen to God, notice greatness, and call it out of them. Don't demand that they become something you want them to be. Encourage them to be anything God wants them to be, and trust that He'll give them the heart and tenacity to follow Him with all their hearts.

> **If you're a mom or a dad, the greatest gift you can give your kids is to call out the greatness God has put in them.**

We need constant reminders of our identity, and thankfully, the Scriptures don't disappoint. Peter wrote, "But you are a chosen people, a royal priesthood, a holy nation, God's special possession, that you may declare the praises of him who called you out of darkness into his wonderful light" (1 Peter 2:9). That's God's message to you: you're royalty, you're a priest who represents God to your spouse, children, friends, neighbors, and coworkers—but especially your children. You're God's treasure. If you grasp these things in any significant way, your heart will swell with joy, and it will burst into praise. And when that happens, you'll display a gospel-shaped identity to the people around you, especially those who look to you as a model for what's important, for messages about who they are, and for an example of how to live.

Your home is a palace that can remind them of God's special calling. It can be an apartment, a mobile home, or a mansion. It doesn't matter. You're King Hiram to your kids. You're building your home to be a refuge and a reminder of the dignity and love God pours out on those who are His. It can remind them every day that they belong to the King who provides shelter from life's storms. Pray Paul's prayer over them. Ask our gracious and powerful God to work His love deep into the crevices of your kids' hearts, so they don't just believe the gospel with their heads, but it transforms them from the inside out.

If you're a teacher, a coach, an aunt or uncle, a grandparent, or a team leader in any organization, you have the unspeakable privilege of speaking truth into the lives of those around you. God has put you there for a reason. It's no mistake, and God will use you to see potential others have missed, to heal hurts, to provide support, and to help them take the next steps on the path God has opened to them.

It's not pride to feel loved, forgiven, and accepted. It's not pride to feel empowered to be and do everything God has for us. Self-pity and self-hatred aren't humility. They're a form of pride because we believe what others say about us instead of what God says about us. For many of us, our identity is shaped more by past wounds and past sins than God's eternal truths. We pray, we study the Scriptures, and we serve, but we live with a nagging sense that we're not worthy. The answer isn't some secular self-help plan. The answer is to trust God to do in us what no one and nothing else can do—transform our identity, so we're thrilled to be called children of the King!

God didn't call us to be great, so we will be known. He has called us to greatness, so others will want to know Him.

Chapter 9

A Higher Calling

A few months after I went to Costa Rica with John, he asked me to join him on his next trip—this time, to Kenya. These weren't sight-seeing trips. They were designed to meet with leaders of the countries to promote a national transformation of values that will then filter into every segment of society. John said, "Scott, it'll be my first trip to Kenya, and I want you to go with me."

It didn't take long for me to answer. I told him, "I'm in. That would be amazing! We have sister churches in Kenya, so it would be a great fit."

He explained, "I can't go to every country and be involved at the level it requires. I need to find a few people who have the same heart, can communicate easily with national leaders, and have the administrative abilities to see all the details come together. Scott, I believe you're one of these people. That's why I want you to go with me on this trip."

John's strategy is to meet with the president or prime minister of a country, and find out what matters to the top leader. Then he hosts roundtables for the leaders in "seven streams" of power: government, business, nonprofit organizations and churches, sports, media and entertainment, education, and health. If the head of the nation doesn't invite him to come, he lacks the shared authority in the eyes of the leaders of the different streams, so he doesn't go. The multiplication process continues throughout each stream as leaders at each level host roundtables for the people who report to them. The numbers can be staggering. For instance, at this point in the small nation of Guatemala, 675,000 people meet in roundtables to infuse everything they do with the values endorsed by the president. And in the schools, about five million sixth- and seventh-grade children are learning and implementing the values of the national leaders that will shape them for true success.

John's goal is to involve ten percent of the population in roundtable discussions. That, author Malcolm Gladwell asserts, is the "tipping point" of broad, structural change in any organization, and it's the necessary threshold for national transformation to happen. The leaders of each stream make it a priority to instill the values throughout their field, and they often invite John to speak at events that kick-start momentum. For instance, when I was with him, he spoke to about eight thousand teachers. At the end of his message, he said, "I'm ending my talk right here, but if any of you want to stay for the next fifteen minutes, I want to tell you about the most important value of my life. I'm honored that leaders introduce me to very important people, and I want to introduce you to the most important person in my life. His name is Jesus. If you're interested, you can stay. If not, thank you so much for coming. You're free to leave now." Quite often, virtually everybody stays, and more than half come forward to profess their faith when John gives the invitation.

After a few days in Kenya, we'd seen God do amazing things. One night when we were all going to our rooms for some much-needed sleep, John put his arm around me and said, "Scott, you were born for this. You're a nation-builder. You were born to bring transformation to nations and individuals. I just want you to know that I see that in you."

I thought my heart might explode, but I just nodded, and we both went to our rooms. If you've read this far in the book, you won't be surprised when I tell you that when I got alone in my room, I questioned what had just happened. I prayed, "Okay, God. Is that John just being nice to me, or is it more than that? Can I really believe what I just heard? Is it from You?"

I sensed God say to me, *I'm speaking through John. I sent him to you like I sent Samuel to David. Since you were young, this is what I've called you to be and do. I'm using John to confirm your calling.*

THE SHIFT

When I got back home, I took a month sabbatical to pray, study, and fast. During the last week, I was at a monastery where there was complete silence. There, I sensed God say, *I'm moving you into a new role as a global pastor. You'll actually be an apostolic spiritual father, but that's not a title people will easily grasp.* He was calling me to be a pastor to pastors and a leader of leaders. Who would fill the role I'd had so long at Oaks Church? I felt sure God had prepared Chris and Cara Railey for the position. They had been on our staff at Oaks Church years before. Since then, Chris had earned his doctorate and had served as the head of the Church Multiplication Network, launching more than three hundred new churches a year. I believed they were a perfect fit, but I didn't want to take anything for granted.

I met with the board when I got home to share what God was telling me to do, and they weren't shocked at all. They agreed to enter a discovery process to see how God would lead us. We weren't going to rush

God. We invited Chris to join our teaching team while he was still doing his work at CMN. He came in one weekend each month to preach on Sunday and to meet with the board and staff behind the scenes. After six months of interviews and prayer, we were convinced that God was calling Chris and Cara to be the next lead pastors at Oaks Church and that Jenni and I were to be the global pastors.

As we planned the installation service for the two transitions, I knew that it would be my responsibility to speak a word of blessing over Chris and Cara and lay hands on them as the new lead pastors, but we needed someone to come and do the same for Jenni and me. I asked the Lord to direct me to the person He wanted to lay hands on us and bless us as global pastors. After prayer, I knew I was to ask John to come in and pray over us.

It was very important to me that this service wasn't just perfunctory, with little more meaning than an announcement and a change of nameplates on my door. I believed it was crucial for this to be a holy moment, one infused with God's presence and power. John knew exactly what I was asking. He'd had three giants of the faith pray over him and ask God to bless his ministry: Bill Bright, Billy Graham, and Bob Hoskins.

I said, "John, you're a spiritual father to me. I'm asking you to come and share the word God gives you about Jenni and me. God used you to confirm this calling, and I'd like you to pray over us to ask God to bless us."

John instantly replied, "I'll be there. It would be an honor."

A week before the service, I was on the phone with John. He was excited. He told me, "Scott, God has given me a word for you and Jenni. It's not in any of my books, and I've never spoken on it before. It's brand new—it's about your being a spiritual father. That's what God is calling you to be. That's what your new role is all about."

On the afternoon before the evening service, I picked up John and Mark Cole at the airport. On the way to our house, Mark smiled and said, "Hey Scott, John has a new message just for you and Jenni. He's been talking about it nonstop all the way here. He's really excited!"

So was I!

We went to our house to have dinner with Chris, Cara, and some of the key leaders in our church. After we ate, John asked if he could meet privately with Jenni and me. We went to another room, and he

handed each of us a beautifully wrapped gift. John explained, "Before you open it, I want to tell you about it. It's a JFK special edition Mont Blanc pen." John often buys Mont Blanc pens to commemorate special events in his travels, and he gave each of us one of the pens. "Do you know why I got that one for you? President Kennedy had a bold vision to go to the moon within a decade. No one knew how it could happen, but his vision moved a nation to do the seemingly impossible. That's the same thing you're doing. You're stepping out of the role of lead pastor tonight. God gave you a bold vision, a vision to do something that hasn't been done before, to build something that hasn't existed. You're going to raise up spiritual fathers and mothers who will raise up spiritual fathers and mothers who will raise up still more spiritual fathers and mothers. You don't know how it will happen, but you're stepping out in faith. Like Abraham, you're being obedient to the call of God. God promised that he'd be the father of many nations. That's what you're becoming. I'm so proud of you."

I opened the box and looked at the pen. On the side it read "Global Pastor."

We drove to the church and prepared for the service. Offstage, I looked over at John as we waited. He was studying his talk notes. By that time, I'd traveled with him to three countries, and I'd never seen him look at his notes.

> **You're going to raise up spiritual fathers and mothers who will raise up spiritual fathers and mothers who will raise up still more spiritual fathers and mothers.**

I teased him, "Hey John, what's the deal with looking at your notes? Are you nervous?"

He put his hand on my shoulder and said, "Let me tell you something, Scott. For most of my talks, I give them so often that I probably mumble them in my sleep. But this is different. This is the first time I've given it, and it'll probably be the last. This is the word God has given me for you."

No more teasing.

When I introduced John to our people, they gave him a standing ovation to show their love and respect. John sat on a stool like he always does, and he began, "There's no way I was going to miss tonight." He turned to Jenni and me and said, "Scott and Jenni, I dearly love you both, and I'm incredibly proud of you." He turned back to the people: "I can tell you right now that Scott and Jenni will be the best global pastors, the most powerful spiritual father and mother combination in America. That's a fact." He turned back to us: "You were born for such a time as this. For over thirty years, you've had an amazing ministry of addition, but now you're stepping into an amazing ministry of multiplication. You're entering a whole new level of your life and ministry, and I'm honored to be here to share this time with you and the people of God. I want to talk about what it means to be a spiritual father. I want to share four ways a father is formed."

I'll summarize the highlights of John's talk, in his words:

First, to be a great father, you have to have a great Father. Notice what the Father said about Jesus at His baptism. As the Holy Spirit descended and landed on Him, the Father spoke: "This is my Son, chosen and marked by my love, delight of my life" (Matthew 3:16-17, MSG).

Jesus heard the Father say what every son and daughter needs to hear:

You belong: "You are My Son."

You are loved: "Chosen and marked by My love."

You are special: "You are the delight of My life."

Second, fatherhood develops by knowing that God is your source. In his letter to the Romans, Paul explained,

We call Abraham "father" not because he got God's attention by living like a saint, but because God made something out of Abraham when he was a nobody. Isn't that what we've always read in Scripture, God saying to Abraham, "I set you up as father of many peoples"? Abraham was first named "father" and then became a father because he dared to trust God to do what only God could do: raise the dead to life, with a word make something out of nothing. When everything was hopeless, Abraham believed anyway, deciding to live not on the basis of what he saw he couldn't do but on what God said he would do. And so he was made father of a multitude of peoples. God himself said to him, "You're going to have a big family, Abraham!"

Abraham didn't focus on his own impotence and say, "It's hopeless. This hundred-year-old body could never father a child." Nor

did he survey Sarah's decades of infertility and give up. He didn't
tiptoe around God's promise asking cautiously skeptical questions.
He plunged into the promise and came up strong, ready for God,
sure that God would make good on what he had said. That's why
it is said, "Abraham was declared fit before God by trusting God
to set him right." But it's not just Abraham; it's also us! The same
thing gets said about us when we embrace and believe the One who
brought Jesus to life when the conditions were equally hopeless.
The sacrificed Jesus made us fit for God, set us right with God."
—Romans 4:17-25 (MSG)

You develop as a father by knowing God is your source. He's for you and with you, and He'll always keep His promises to you. It's one thing to announce to everyone that you are a father after you have a kid or two to prove it. But it's quite another thing to say, "God already sees me for who I am to be—even before I can see who I am to be. I'm a father, not because I have kids, but because God says I am."

It's wonderful to believe in yourself, but it's more wonderful to realize how much God believes in you.

We also develop as fathers when we focus on God instead of ourselves. That's what Abraham did. God told them they'd have a family as numerous as the stars in the sky, and He said it when they still hadn't had a single child.

Scott, I want you to focus tonight on the fact that you are about to father a great multitude of people. This is just the beginning. Scott and Jenni, God is saying that you are going to have a big family. You are going to have a lot of children. Don't focus on the things you don't have. Focus your whole attention on who God says you are becoming.

Third, fatherhood thrives by practicing good father behaviors. Every year I ask God to give me a word for the year, and I focus my heart and my thoughts for the whole year on that word. Some people ask, "John, why do you ask God for just a word?" It's because I don't think I can handle an entire sentence! And sometimes a word is too much for me to handle. This year, the word God gave me is "father." As I prayed over this word, I realized it's the same word God has given you, Scott.

As a father, I . . .

Bless and empower others.

Unconditionally love them.

Revel in their success.

Birth spiritual babies.

Provide fatherly counsel.

Oaks Church, you are sending Scott and Jenni out to be global pastors and raise up spiritual fathers and mothers around the world. You are such a mature people. Most churches don't have the foresight and vision to do such a thing. I want you to know that you are going to be a participant in all that God is about to do through them. It's going to be amazing!

And fourth, fatherhood culminates when moral authority is recognized by others. Moral authority is the recognition that a leader's influence is greater than titles or positions. It's only given by those who have experienced the blessings and benefits of being with that leader.

Scott and Jenni, as we pray over you tonight, we aren't just installing you into a new position; we're here for something weightier than a title—we're praying that you'll have moral authority.

Moral authority happens when a leader possesses competence, courage, consistency, and character. As the leader of Israel, David earned moral authority. The kingdom had been divided, but both sides recognized that David was (and had been) their true leader. The passage reads:

> *Then all Israel assembled before David at Hebron. "Look at us," they said. "We're your very flesh and blood. In the past, yes, even while Saul was king, you were the real leader of Israel. God told you, 'You will shepherd my people Israel; you are to be the ruler of my people Israel.'" When all the elders of Israel came to the king at Hebron, David made a covenant with them in the presence of God at Hebron. Then they anointed David king over Israel exactly as God had commanded through Samuel. —1 Chronicles 11:1-3 (MSG)*

Notice what they said: "Even while Saul was king, you were the real leader of Israel." That's moral authority!

John ended his message by asking Jenni and me three questions: "As a child of God, do you feel secure in Him?"

We answered, "Yes, we do."

"Do you recognize God as your source of service?"

We answered, "Yes, we do."

"Will you practice good father behaviors?"

We answered, "Yes, we will."

John then anointed Jenni and me with oil and laid hands on us. He prayed, "Father, we stand amazed at how far You have brought these two. They are secure in Your love, they recognize that You are their source, and they have practiced good fathering behaviors—proving they are worthy of this prayer and installation. So we anoint them with power and favor that they might have recognition and followership around the world." He then addressed the two of us and said, "I anoint you in the name of the Father, the Son, and the Holy Spirit. Now become the father and mother God has birthed in your spirit."

John wasn't quite finished. He asked Mark Cole to bring something to the stage. It was a golden baton resting on a glass stand. He read the words on the plaque: "To Scott and Jenni Wilson, installed as Global Pastor of Oaks Church, June 26, 2020." Then he turned to me and said, "When we were in Kenya, I put my arm around you and said, 'You're a nation-builder. God has called you to lead leaders.' I'm passing a baton to you. It's your time. Run the race. Run the race."

John left the stage. I told our people, "Have you ever had a time when you thought, *It can't get any better than this,* and then it does? That's what you're about to experience. As great as that was, I'm honored to bring Chris and Cara Railey up to lead this church. They're going to take Oaks Church to a new level of power and impact."

As a part of installing Chris, I gave him a ring with three parts. I told him, "This part is me, this part is you, and the third part is the pastor who will come after you. As you look at the ring every day, remember what you've received, what you have, and what you'll give to the next leader of this church. God called himself 'the God of Abraham, Isaac, and Jacob.' That means God is the Father of a father of a father of a father of the nation that blessed the entire world. That's how God identifies Himself, and that's where you and I fit in His plans to bless the world."

I turned to the people and said, "Whether you've been in this church for thirty years or thirty days, you've heard me tell the story: One night I had a dream of preaching on a platform to a great audience as God did miracles and thousands were saved. I looked down and realized I was standing on my father's shoulders. Today, after twenty years as the pastor of this church, Jenni and I are stepping off the platform, and we're taking our place under the platform, so Chris and Cara can stand on our shoulders. We're moving into a role where we'll invite other pastors around the world to stand on our shoulders, and we'll live the rest of our lives with people standing on our shoulders. Our lives won't be defined by what we've done on the platform but by what others do as they stand on our shoulders."

ALL OF US

A friend of mine asked, "That's a fantastic, glorious story, but Scott, that's your story. How do the rest of us relate to it?"

I told him, "I'm nothing special. Not at all. But God considers me to be incredibly special because I belong to Him. I'm nothing on my own, but in Christ, I'm a child of the King. That's how God sees me, and He sees you exactly the same way. Yes, this is my story, but God has something wonderful for all of us if we'll listen to Him and choose to follow wherever He leads. That process almost certainly isn't what we expected. When I was in my twenties, I wanted to be great, I wanted to be known, but God had to change my heart so that I want, more than anything, to make Him known and for people to realize His greatness and grace. God will give each of us a dream—maybe not one we wake up to in the middle of the night, but one that He shapes in our hearts . . . an unmistakable calling we can't ignore. It begins, as my father taught me, with loving God and loving people. If we get that right, everything else will follow. The moment I said, 'I'm in for that,' God said, 'Good, but your life isn't going to be what you expected. Your calling isn't about what you do on a platform; it's about what you do under the platform as people stand on your shoulders.'"

Some have wondered if I'm too young to be a spiritual father. The role isn't about age; it's about heart and calling. I've had that role since I was in my twenties. I believe it's the primary calling of every believer: to pour ourselves into others, so they excel in fulfilling whatever God puts on their hearts. There is no greater joy. My success isn't defined by what I do but by how I can help others do great things for God . . . and sometimes, to just hang in there with God when the going gets tough. That's part of being a spiritual father, too.

> **Yes, this is my story, but God has something wonderful for all of us if we'll listen to Him and choose to follow wherever He leads.**

I've had to learn, the hard way, that God values faithfulness over talent. When we choose to obey God day after day after day, the cumulative effect is a life that reflects the heart and life of Jesus. We don't show up to be served but to serve. We don't demand a position, but we're humble enough to dive in wherever there's a need. We don't care about our glory, but we delight in making God famous. Being a spiritual father or mother isn't weird. It just means we care more about the people coming after us than our own power and prestige. No matter your age, your background, or your title, that's God's calling for all of us.

It's the story of Jesus written on countless hearts in generation after generation.

I was thrilled that John Maxwell came to speak and pray over Jenni and me when we were installed in our new role, but let me be honest, the second part of the service, when we left the stage and symbolically went under the platform, so Chris and Cara could stand on our shoulders was even more fulfilling. It's what I live for!

God is amazing. He's always at work, even when we can't see it. He has purposes that are far higher, love that's far deeper, and a vision that's far wider than anything I can imagine . . . and He has invited you and me to be His partners. What a privilege!

God the Father has given me a revelation of His will at each step in my life. He opened my eyes to His love, and He confirmed my identity as His child. I was discouraged more times than I can count, so I'd give these pieces of advice to everyone on the journey:

When you feel rejected, don't give up. Trust the timing of the Lord. Trust the process of the Lord. Expect God to show up . . . He will.

Epilogue
Lasting Impact

Dr. Chand and John continue to be spiritual fathers to me, and I treasure my relationship with them. In the past year, I've valued their encouragement even more. It has been a whirlwind: my father died of Alzheimer's disease, God has called me to be a spiritual father, and He orchestrated the transition for me to become the global pastor at Oaks Church. These experiences have brought me back, again and again, to my dad's impact on my life. I want to end the book with more of the story of how his love, truth, and support have made me the person I am today. I've shared much of this in my book, *Parenting with Purpose*, but it bears another look now.

During my entire childhood, until the day I could drive, my dad took me to school each day. He wasn't just the driver; he was a mentor and teacher for my brothers and me. Each day, we recited the week's memory verse until we could say it together. As we neared the school, he asked each of us to pray for our day, and before we got out, he prayed for us: "God, touch my sons. Let them know how much You love them and care about them. Let them be the men You want them to be today, to love You and others as young men of God. And Lord, give them wisdom in all their work and favor with their teachers and friends. Keep Your hand on them and let them fulfill Your purpose today." Our daily ritual wasn't complete until two more things happened: Dad asked us to quote our family verse, Psalm 19:14, and as the car opened and we sprinted out, Dad called to each of us, "I love you, Scott! I love you, Brent! I love you, Bracy!"

Back then, I didn't realize how special those times were. I wanted to listen to the radio on the way to school . . . or tease Brent about the girl he'd been talking to the day before . . . or talk about our next football or baseball game . . . anything but Scripture and prayer! But today, I see the beauty of my dad's gift to us each morning.

As I've described in the early chapters, Dad had a profound impact on me as a young leader. He encouraged me, redirected me, and challenged my impatience. I couldn't have asked for a better dad or a better pastor.

When he was diagnosed with Alzheimer's disease, it wasn't a surprise to any of us who were close to him. We'd seen a gradual decline for some time. It wasn't long before he needed more care than Mom could give him at home. His first week in the memory care facility was really hard on all of us. We knew we'd passed a significant point in our relationship with him. No more wishful thinking that he'd suddenly get better. No more denial that it wasn't really that bad. One day that week, I walked into his room, and he didn't recognize me. I stood next to him for several minutes while he talked to the nurse. I was heartbroken. After a while, the nurse smiled and said, "Mr. Wilson, who is that man standing next to you?"

Dad looked at me and said, "Oh, I can tell he's a great guy."

The nurse asked, "Yes, but who is he?"

Dad stared at me and shook his head. "He looks familiar, but I can't quite place him."

The nurse suggested, "Take another look."

Dad was getting frustrated with her. He told her, "If you want to know, why don't you ask him yourself?"

I didn't wait for the question. I got down on his level and looked him in the eyes. I told him, "Dad, listen to my voice. You know me."

A sudden look of realization flashed on his face. "Scott, is that you? Is that you, son?"

Tears came to my eyes. "Yes, Dad. It's me."

He couldn't stop. "You're here! You're here!" He turned to the nurse and told her, "This is my son!"

I sat on his bed. We hugged each other and talked. Quite often, I wasn't sure what he was saying. The sentences, and sometimes the words, didn't seem to connect. As he talked, I thought about how he had taught me the Bible, how he had prayed so fervently for me and taught me to pray, how his life had been characterized by a steadfast, immovable faith in God, how well he had loved Mom, Brent, Bracy, and me, and what a wonderful pastor he had been to the people in our church. Two powerful emotions welled up in me: deep sadness and profound gratitude.

In the months since his funeral, I've thought a lot about what it means for a father or mother to implant an identity in a child. My father was an incredible dad, but I still have had plenty of "daddy issues." I think it's inherent in being fallen people in a fallen world—we can't escape it. We need a Father who is even better than my dad, one who heals every wound, speaks hope into every disappointment, forgives no matter what we've done, and has a purpose for us that's far beyond anything we can imagine. Thankfully, we have a heavenly Father just like that. He's the one who gives us a strong, secure identity based on His unconditional love instead of our performance. He's the one whose "everlasting arms" always hold us.

We need a Father who is even better than my dad, one who heals every wound, speaks hope into every disappointment, forgives no matter what we've done, and has a purpose for us that's far beyond anything we can imagine.

A friend who has a background in counseling told me that some of those who read about my relationship with my dad will have fond memories of the love their fathers showered on them, but for others, the story will surface long-buried, intense feelings of hurt, shame, and outrage. They remember the abuse or abandonment, the harsh words or the painful silence, and the old emotions rise again. He explained that this can be a very helpful, healing moment if those people are honest about their wounds, find a safe person who encourages them to grieve their losses, and experience God's tender love, maybe for the first time. The contrast between their earthly parents and their heavenly Father is stark and true, and healing painful memories is essential.

It's certainly not my intention to torture people by reminding them of the love they missed when they were kids, but perhaps telling my story will provide an opportunity for at least some people to pour out their hearts to God and a safe person . . . and experience God's compassion, kindness, and presence.

In my thoughts about identity, I've gone back again and again to that moment at the Jordan when Jesus went into the water to be baptized. The voice came from heaven: "You are my beloved Son, whom I love; with you I am well pleased" (Luke 3:22). This statement of a strong, secure identity was made before Jesus had preached a single sermon, chosen a single disciple, or healed a single person. The Father gave Jesus three things all of our hearts yearn for:

Identity—"You are my Son."

Affection—"Whom I love."

Affirmation—"I'm well pleased with You."

On that day in the memory care facility in the first moments when Dad didn't recognize me, he couldn't give me these three gifts. He had given them before, and they meant the world to me. That's why it hurt so much. I wanted him to instantly tell everybody within the range of hearing, "This is my son, Scott! Isn't he terrific?" When he finally recognized me, it took everything in me to keep from bursting out in sobs. It felt so good to be claimed as his own, to be loved, and to know he was pleased with me.

God has made us so that only His recognition, affection, and affirmation can fill the hole in our hearts and give us the security we long for. Again and again, I need to hear the Father tell me what He said to Jesus: "Scott, you are my son, whom I love; with you I am well pleased." And I need to be assured that His affection isn't conditioned on how good a husband, dad, friend, or leader I am. Apart from my performance, I need to hear Him shout so that all of heaven hears: "Scott, you

> **Apart from my performance, I need to hear Him shout so that all of heaven hears: "Scott, you belong to Me! You're mine, and I love you more than you can know!"**

belong to Me! You're mine, and I love you more than you can know!" That kind of love forms an identity that humbles us and energizes us to do everything we can to honor our Father.

After Dad recognized me and we hugged and talked for a while, I asked him if he'd like to play the piano for me. There was one near his room. He smiled and said, "Oh, no, son. I don't want to waste time on that. I just want to sit here and talk to you." We continued to talk. Several times he leaned over and kissed me on the cheek. He told me over and over how much he loved me. When he spoke, he had tears in his eyes. That's the depth of his love for me. It meant so much for those heartfelt words to come from my dad, but I also need to hear the Father say this to me. He does, but can I hear Him?

After our visit, I got in my car and wept. I sensed the Lord wrap His arms around me and say, *While you were hugging your dad, I was hugging you. When you're grieving over your dad, I'm still hugging you. When you're scared about what the future might bring, I'm hugging you. When you feel alone or hurt or ashamed or angry, I'm hugging you and telling you, "Scott, you're my son. I love you, and I'm so pleased with you."*

I have a hunger and thirst for affirmation. I don't think I'm alone in that. Before Dad's memory faded too much, I took him to lunch at one of his favorite restaurants. We talked about the tragedy of the kids on the border who had been separated from their parents. He told me about his plans to build two dozen schools and churches to care for people at the border. He told me, "We'll put a sign next to the border that says, 'Welcome to your window of opportunity: Life School and Oaks Church.'" Here was a man who had lost his mind, but he hadn't lost his vision.

When we got in the car, I didn't drive away immediately. I turned to Dad and asked, "Dad, do you think I'm doing okay with the church?"

He began to cry. He told me, "Son, God is blessing the church like I've never seen before. It's beyond my dreams, and son, you're a wonderful leader. You're anointed. You're my pastor. I couldn't be prouder of you."

I said, "Dad, would you pray for me that God would help me be all He wants me to be?"

He leaned over, put his hands on my head and prayed: "Father, touch my son. Bless my son. Help him be everything You want him to be. Help him walk in alignment with You, and keep him close to You. Use him and empower him to completely fulfill the calling on his life. Amen."

He kissed me and hugged me. He said again, "I'm so proud of you, Scott."

I'll never forget that moment, but it's not enough to fill the gaping hole in my soul. I want to hear those words from my dad, but I desperately need to hear them from my heavenly Father. And I hear them. Yes, I hear them.

I often return to the Father's words to Jesus at His baptism, and because we're "in Christ," it's the same message to us. Some people have wondered if we can apply the Father's statement to Jesus to us. Yes, we can. The Scriptures are clear: We're "in Christ" in His death, so His sacrifice applies to our sins. We're "in Christ" in His life, so His righteousness is credited to us. We're "in Christ" in His resurrection, so we share in His power. And we're "in Christ" in His ascension to the throne, so we have His delegated authority as royal children.

But that may seem too abstract for some people. There's more. Twice on the night He was betrayed, Jesus made astounding statements about our identity as beloved children of God. He explained that He loves us as much as the Father loves Him: "As the Father has loved me, so have I loved you" (John 15:9). And in His prayer that night, Jesus said that when we're assured of our identity, we'll realize the Father loves us as much as He loves Jesus: "Then the world will know that you sent me and have loved them even as you have loved me" (John 17:23). How's that for assurance of God's love?

My dad's death has left a hole in my life. I miss him so much. As I think about him and pray, I sense God saying, *I know you miss him, but I'm with you. I love you, and I'm pleased with you. I'll get you through this. Your dad is with Me, and he's not just okay—he's exactly where he's always wanted to be!*

Our sense of identity is the lid on our personal growth. If we're wracked by self-doubt, fear, and shame, we'll either be hesitant or impulsive . . . or both! But when God opens our hearts to truly experience the wonder of His love—and be convinced of it—the lid is removed. We'll become the people God created us to be, and we'll be the fathers, mothers, sons, daughters, friends, mentors, and leaders He wants us to be.

Let it sink in:

"You are My beloved child."

"I love you more than you can know."

"I'm so proud of you."

Believe it. It's true. It's God's message to you today and every day.

About The Author

For more than thirty years, Scott Wilson grew Oaks Church into a thriving local ministry with high global impact. Under his leadership, the Oaks has served thousands of families in the South Dallas area and has raised up and sent out hundreds of successful leaders, both nationally and internationally. Having seen the valuable impact of providing a spiritual covering to many church leaders, Scott founded The 415 Leadership to raise up spiritual fathers and mothers with a vision that every pastor should have spiritual parents. He also founded Ready Set Grow, a ministry to help churches break through their growth barriers by sharing his own experience and best-in-class partners. Scott has written many books and is a sought-after speaker on personal, spiritual, and organizational growth and leadership. Scott and his wife, Jenni, have been married since 1990 and have three sons and two daughters-in-law: Dillon and Holly, Hunter and Emily, and Dakota. Their first grandson, Teddy, was born in July, 2021.

LEADERS

OUR CEILING. YOUR FLOOR.

415 Leaders multiplies spiritual fathers and mothers to multiply churches. The Apostle Paul said, "You have many teachers, but you don't have many fathers." We think that is just as true today as it was when it was written. It's time to do something about it. The missing component of our church multiplication models today is the presence of spiritual fathers and mothers, experienced pastors who carry the heart of the Father and are committed to the long-term success of the next generation of church leaders. While institutional support is helpful, there is no substitute for the enduring, relational investment of healthy, seasoned pastors. Time after time, we have heard from church planters and young pastors that they feel alone and ill-equipped, desperate not only for the relationships that a mentor and peer group could provide, but also for the wisdom of a leader who

has navigated the personal, family, and organizational challenges they face. For the Church to be effective in the future, we must create solutions to not only raise up its next leaders from our congregations today, but we must also provide models to leverage the untapped wisdom and relational capacity of healthy, seasoned pastors. By 2030, we believe the Lord has given us a plan to raise up 1,000 spiritual fathers and mothers and plant over 4,000 churches together.

"My wife Christina and I planted Overflow City Church near Washington, D.C., in the fall of 2018. Having a spiritual father to help us through this process has been a gamechanger. Without one, the journey would have been much more challenging, and I feel like we wouldn't have had the tools and resources we needed. Our spiritual parents have had a significant impact on our personal growth and the growth of our team. It's so great to know we are not alone in this"

—Paul and Christina Hanfere
Overflow City Church

To become a spiritual father and mother or to connect with a spiritual father and mother, go to 415leaders.com.

Ready Set Grow

A customized coaching journey to help you grow your church

There's a weight that comes with being a pastor. It feels intense because you know what's on the line—hundreds if not thousands of souls hanging in the balance. Knowing what you and your church do next will affect their eternity.

Many pastors are just trying to survive and get through the week. They feel scattered. Struggling to focus. Starting to doubt they've got what it takes to lead. You're not alone. We've been where you are now, and we've made it to the other side.

The Inner Circle is a three-year customized coaching journey giving you everything you need to know to grow a church and become a high-performing pastor.

On this 36-month journey, you will be part of an exclusive group of high-performing pastors coached by Scott Wilson and his own elite growth team to consistently

discover the next mountain to take, **design** the plan to get there, and **deliver** results you need to grow your church.

Deliverables: What You Get When You Join The Inner Circle

- Kickoff Retreat
- Activator Certification in the Intentional Growth Planning System
- Comprehensive Resources Suite
- Monthly Group Cohort Calls
- Quarterly Results Assessments
- Lead Pastor Dashboard to stay focused on High ROI Activities
- Church Domain Dashboard to stay focused on the 6 Essential Domains for Growth
- Personal access to our Inner Circle Team of Experts
- Duplicatable Strategic Growth Planning System
- Your own Personal Success Guide

Inner Circle Success Guides have comprehensive ministry experience and background. They are highly proficient in Inner Circle's coaching, application and assessment framework. This combination ensures a successful Inner Circle journey for you and your church.

To apply for the Inner Circle, go to rsgleaders.com.

Ready Set Grow

U N I V E R S I T Y

Members will have exclusive access to the following benefits:

**LIVE MONTHLY
COACHING SESSIONS**

With Scott Wilson

**MONTHLY GUEST
INFLUENCER SESSIONS**

Curated by Scott Wilson

**RESOURCES IN THE
MAIL**

Curated by Scott Wilson

**BEST OF SCOTT
LIBRARY**

CONTENT ARCHIVES

Curated by Scott Wilson

MEMBERS DISCOUNT

To other related products and events

**Go to SCOTTWILSONLEADERS.COM
to get 30 DAY FREE trial access to
RSG UNIVERSITY ($29.00/mo after trial ends)**

Other books by Scott Wilson

HOW DO PEOPLE PERCEIVE YOU?

In *Impact: Releasing the Power of Influence*, you will be challenged and encouraged regarding how to become a strong, loving leader. That is not only what God wants you to be, it's also what your peers and mentors need you to be. In these pages, you'll find timeless and invaluable guidance on crucial topics: earning respect, creating 10x moments, finding your values, building relationships, and more! If you desire to make an impact on others, you must love others the way the Lord loves them—and you. Join global pastor and conference leader Scott Wilson on an incredible journey by leaving your comfort zone and learning how to multiply your IMPACT!

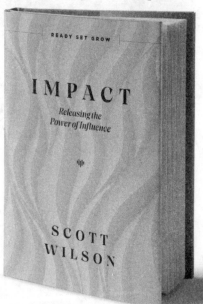

scottwilsonimpact.com

7 KEYS TO RAISING UP WORLD-CHANGERS

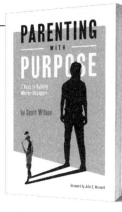

God has given us the most sweeping vision the world has ever known—to make disciples of people in every nation on earth and make a difference wherever we go. And He has en-trusted us with the people we need to equip to fulfill that vision—our children and grandchildren. The stakes couldn't be higher, and our role couldn't be more important. In this book, Pastor Scott Wilson encourages us to have a God-sized dream for our impact on the next generation, a dream that's far bigger than we can accomplish on our own, so we need to trust God more than ever . . . and a dream that reaches into generations to come. With warmth, humor, biblical teaching, and practical insights, this book equips all of us—parents, grandparents, teachers, coaches, and mentors—to instill God's heart into the children in our lives. That's His plan, and we are His strategy.

parentingwithpurposebook.com

PRAYING...IN THE SPIRIT, WITH UNDERSTANDING, AND IN AGREEMENT

In this book, Pastor Scott Wilson explains how God led him and his church to experience far more of His mind, His heart, and His direction than ever before. And it's not a secret. Church staff teams, small groups, couples, families, and congregations can tap more deeply into the presence of the Spirit. Pastor Scott tells the story about how God led him to the concepts of "P3 prayer," the biblical foundation of it, and the powerful process that enables all of us to listen as God speaks and "be filled with all the fullness of God." Do you want God to revolutionize your prayer life?

p3book.com

ADDITIONAL RESOURCES

RSGleaders.com

ΛVΛIL+